"A unique look at a unique culture. If you're trying to figure the Japanese out, this book provides another important piece of the puzzle."
—Terrie Lloyd, Founder & Publisher, *J@pan Inc.*;
CEO, LINC Media, Tokyo

"Among the numerous books by foreigners on the intricate Japanese mindscapes and businessscapes, Boyé Lafayette De Mente's *KATA: The Key to Understanding & Dealing with the Japanese!* is undoubtedly the most informative and eye-opening; it is rich in exploratory insight and provocative wisdom."
—Dr. Tae-Chang Kim, President, Institute
for the Integrated Study of Future Generations, Kyoto

"In working with the most traditional sectors of the Japanese economy (real estate and construction), where few foreigners ever penetrate, I have experienced the gorge of misunderstanding between Japan and the rest of the world. *KATA* explains the rationale for Japanese behavior and fills in the blanks for everyone, including long-term foreign residents."
—James Fink, General Manager, Colliers Halifax, Tokyo

"I have been acting as a bridge between Japanese and foreign businessmen for nearly forty years. This book says what I have been trying to say all those years."
—Tokuo Maruoka, Former Director,
Price Waterhouse Japan; Founder & Chairman, Comito Inc., Tokyo

"Even long-time students of Japan will find the book illuminating and thought-provoking."
—Sam Jameson, former Tokyo Bureau Chief of the
Chicago Tribune and the *Los Angeles Times*

"KATA explains the rationale for Japanese behavior and fills in the blanks for everyone, including long-term foreign residents."
—James Fink, General Manager, Colliers Halifax, Tokyo

T0161148

KATA as the Key to Understanding the Japanese

型

JAPAN
A Guide to Traditions, Customs and Etiquette

BOYÉ LAFAYETTE DE MENTE

Revised by Geoff Botting

TUTTLE Publishing

Tokyo | Rutland, Vermont | Singapore

ABOUT TUTTLE
"Books to Span the East and West"

Our core mission at Tuttle Publishing is to create books which bring people together one page at a time. Tuttle was founded in 1832 in the small New England town of Rutland, Vermont (USA). Our fundamental values remain as strong today as they were then—to publish best-in-class books informing the English-speaking world about the countries and peoples of Asia. The world has become a smaller place today and Asia's economic, cultural and political influence has expanded, yet the need for meaningful dialogue and information about this diverse region has never been greater. Since 1948, Tuttle has been a leader in publishing books on the cultures, arts, cuisines, languages and literatures of Asia. Our authors and photographers have won numerous awards and Tuttle has published thousands of books on subjects ranging from martial arts to paper crafts. We welcome you to explore the wealth of information available on Asia at **www. tuttlepublishing.com**.

Published by Tuttle Publishing, an imprint of Periplus Editions (HK) Ltd.

www.tuttlepublishing.com

Text © Boyé Lafayette De Mente, 2017
First Tuttle edition, 2013

All rights reserved. No part of this publication may be reproduced or utilized in any form or by any means, electronic or mechanical, including photocopying, recording, or by any information storage and retrieval system, without prior written permission of the publisher.

ISBN 978-4-8053-1442-5
(*Previously published as KATA, Isbn 978-0-8048-3386-8, LCC Card No. 2004267142 and ISBN 978-4-8053-1105-9 (for sale in Japan only)*)

22 21 20 19   10 9 8 7 6 5 4
Printed in China   1907RR

TUTTLE PUBLISHING® is a registered trademark of Tuttle Publishing, a division of Periplus Editions (HK) Ltd.

Distributed by:

North America, Latin America and Europe
Tuttle Publishing
364 Innovation Drive
North Clarendon, VT 05759-9436
Tel: 1 (802) 773 8930
Fax: 1 (802) 773 6993
info@tuttlepublishing.com
www.tuttlepublishing.com

Japan
Tuttle Publishing
Yaekari Building 3F, 5-4-12 Osaki
Shinagawa-ku, Tokyo 141-0032
Tel: (81) 3 5437 0171
Fax: (81) 3 5437 0755
sales@tuttle.co.jp
www.tuttle.co.jp

Asia Pacific
Berkeley Books Pte Ltd
3 Kallang Sector, #04-01/02,
Singapore 349278
Tel: (65) 6280 1330
Fax: (65) 6280 6290
inquiries@periplus.com.sg
www.tuttlepublishing.com

Contents

3

Kata in Japan Today 80

4
Kata in Business 130

5
Weaknesses of the Japanese System 182

Front cover Fushimi Inari Shrine in Kyoto. The shrine is associated with businesses and commerce. Business people routinely gates to the shrines in hopes of achieving financial success.

Page 2 Two of Japan's best-known symbols: cherry blossoms in bloom with Mount Fuji in the background.

Foreword

Dispelling the Enigma Myth of Japan

TRADITIONALLY, the Japanese were an enigma to the West. When Westerners first encountered the Japanese in the 16th century, the differences in their attitudes and behavior were so profound and conspicuous that these early visitors were either shocked or delighted, depending on the circumstances.

The Japanese not only bathed daily, both genders bathed together. Prostitution districts were a part of the national infrastructure. Regular sexual release was regarded as essential for one's physical and mental health.

Samurai warriors were legally permitted to kill anyone on the spot who ignored rules of etiquette. The Shogunate government and provincial lords engaged the services of *ninja* (neen-jah), or professional assassins. It was a capital offense to teach foreigners the Japanese language. From the late 1630s to the mid-1850s, any Japanese who left the country and returned was subject to the death penalty.

The Japanese routinely appeared to be incapable of telling the truth, even in situations where there was nothing to be gained from lying. Facts were ignored, and "face" was more important than life itself.

These customs and mind-set resulted in Westerners assuming that there was something mysterious in the makeup of the Japanese character that accounted for their extra-ordinary behavior. This led to the creation of a "mystery of the Orient" myth that became a primary theme in Western writings on Japan, profoundly influencing all of our relations with the Japanese.

To complicate matters further, the Japanese themselves historically suffered from a similar malady that might be called the "mystery of the West." Their view of the Western world was just as distorted as the Westerners' view of them.

Noting this phenomenon in the late 1960s, Japanologist George H. Lambert observed that they (the Japanese) often reacted to Westerners on the basis of old and well-preserved stereotypes with behavioral patterns that were incompatible with their normal conduct. "Thus," he added, "it often happens that we are reacting to abnormal Japanese behavior that is in itself a reaction to us."

In fact, the Japanese have always been among the most explainable people on Earth due to their deeply entrenched custom of formalized role-playing, which influenced every aspect of their attitudes and behavior. The "mystery" that blocked the Westerners' view and understanding of the Japanese was simply their own veil of cultural myopia; their own ignorance of the essence of the Japanese way of thinking and doing things.

Today, despite the fact that Japan has become the world's third largest economy and the variety and volume of exchanges between Japan and the rest of the world are awesome, culture-based problems continue to cause misunderstandings and mistakes—by both Japanese and their foreign counterparts.

There have, of course, been dramatic changes in Japan's culture since the 1960s, but foreigners typically read too much into these changes. The country and the people have a Western facade that Westerners tend to take at face value, only to be brought up short when things do not go the way they expect.

The cultural differences between most Japanese and Westerners remain deep and enduring, and can only be dealt with through understanding, tolerance and well-intentioned compromise.

But it is not so much cultural differences on an individual level that separate the Japanese and others. It is the power and influence of "the system"—a combination of traditional culture and bureaucracy taken to the extreme—that dominate Japan, and prevents the Japanese from doing things differently—from doing things they know should be done, and would like to do, in business as well as in their personal affairs.

The challenge for foreigners dealing with the Japanese continues to be relating to their cultural and social mind-set in the context of the system in which they live. That is what "Kata" is all about.

—Boyé Lafayette De Mente

Introduction

What Makes the Japanese *Japanese*?

B Y ANY WORLD world standard, the Japanese are an extraordinary people. Their success in turning a small chain of resource-poor islands into a major economic power in less than three decades is proof of that.

The fact that the postwar "Miracle of Japan" would not have happened without significant contributions from the United States and Western Europe, along with a variety of other external factors, certainly tempers, but does not in any way, negate the accomplishments of the Japanese.

Japan's modern history has been a record of accomplishments, beginning with its transformation from a feudalistic kingdom of sword-carrying warriors, shopkeepers and peasants in 1868 to a world-class military power by 1895.

The special character and ability of the Japanese were recognized by more astute Western visitors even before Japan's feudal age ended. American ship captain Henry Holmes, who made a number of trips to Japan prior to its opening to the West, noted in his journal, "They (the Japanese) will surprise the world!"

And surprise the world they have—in ways that have ranged from marvelous to shocking.

The first Westerners of record to visit Japan arrived by accident in 1543, blown off course by the winds of a typhoon. These Westerners—Portuguese traders who were passengers on a Chinese junk—introduced guns, tobacco, and venereal disease to the Japanese.

The next foreign visitor of note was a Jesuit priest named Francis Xavier, who arrived from the Portuguese settlement

Japanese paper lanterns, or *chochin*, have been used in modern-day Japan to decorate shrines, temples, businesses, and drinking spots.

of Macau in 1549 determined to introduce the Japanese to Christianity.

Over the next several decades other missionaries and foreign traders by the hundreds descended upon Japan, eager to win minds or make fortunes.

The Japanese were unlike any people previously encountered by the globe-circling Europeans of the 16th century. They were roughly divided into two large classes—an elite sword-wearing warrior class, and the common people. Their social system was based on vertical ranking within a military dictatorship headed by shoguns, and a highly sophisticated, rigidly enforced etiquette that governed all inter-personal relationships.

Male members of the warrior class, which made up about 10 percent of the population, were fierce fighters who tended to be aggressive and arrogant. The common people were characteristically polite, kind, generous, hospitable, trustworthy, and diligent. And most of them were rice and vegetable farmers. Others were fishermen, craftsmen, and merchants. Members of the warrior class administered the laws of the country for the shogunate government.

This well-defined Japanese way of life, already more than a thousand years old at the beginning of the 16th century, was an elaborately refined combination of Shinto, Buddhist, Confucian, and Taoist precepts that the Imperial Court, the Shogun's Court, and the warrior class had molded into a unique culture which distinguished the Japanese from all other Asians, and especially made them different from Westerners.

These cultural differences intrigued and frustrated the first foreigners to arrive in Japan, many of whom spent a great deal of time trying to figure out why the Japanese thought and behaved the way they did. No one solved the enigma, although a great deal of insight into Japanese behavior was gained in the attempt.

In the 1630s, fearing outside interference and eventual colonization attempts, Japan's feudal rulers expelled all foreign residents and closed the country to all except for one small Dutch trading post that was moved to *Dejima*, which was a minuscule man-made islet in built in the bay of Nagasaki. This isolated Dutch outpost was allowed one trade-ship visit per year. With the exception of an occasional ship from China or Korea, all other travel to and from the country was strictly prohibited, with the penalty for breaking this law being death. The hundreds of Japanese who were abroad at that time were barred from ever returning home.

This ban remained in force until the 1850s, when the United States sent a fleet of warships into Tokyo Bay to pry the country open at the behest of American whalers, trading companies, and others who wanted to prevent Russia, England, and other countries from gaining an advantage over the United States.

In the years that followed, a flood of foreigners poured into Japan, some of them invited as technicians and teachers by the Meiji government that replaced the shogunate, and others seeking the usual business profits and religious converts.

Over the next one hundred years, Japan was studied, analyzed, and dissected by thousands of foreign residents trying to understand the culture and devise ways for effectively dealing with the Japanese. Some of these early "old Japan hands" produced memorable books about the character and customs of the Japanese. These books are still read to this day.

Japan's miraculous recovery from the devastation of World War II and its rapid climb to world power status resulted in massive new efforts to describe and explain the attitudes and behavior of the Japanese to the rest of the world—and in particular to explain why and how the Japanese were able to achieve extraordinary economic success in such a short period of time.

While most of the special traits and talents of the Japanese have now been accurately described by foreign businessmen, writers, and scholars, no one has yet explained where these special traits and talents came from and how they became an integral part of Japanese culture.

I believe the answer to this puzzle lies in the special acculturation and training techniques called *shikata* (she-kah-tah)—or *kata* (kah-tah) when used in compound terms—developed and used by the Japanese over the centuries. This book looks at the origin, nature, use, and influence of the kata factor in Japanese life.

I am greatly indebted to Dan Nakatsu, who spent many years in Japan as an airline and advertising executive, for encouraging me to focus on the kata factor in Japanese culture, and to old Japan hands Ken Butler, William K. Nichoson, Davis Barrager, Joseph P. Schmelzeis, Jr.—and several others who prefer not to be named—for reading the first draft of this book and making many suggestions for its improvement.

1

The Kata Factor

Japan's Secret Weapon

SHIKATA (she-kah-tah) is one of the most used and most important words in the Japanese language. It means "way of doing things," with special emphasis on the form and order of the process. The root meaning of *shi* is a combination of "support" and "serve" in the sense of an inferior supporting and serving a superior. *Kata*, by itself, is usually translated as "form."

Some of the more common uses of kata include *yomi kata* (yoh-me kah-tah), or "way of reading"; *tabe kata* (tah-bay kah-tah), or "way of eating"; *kaki kata* (kah-kee kah-tah), or "way of writing"; *kangae kata* (kahn-guy kah-tah), or "way of thinking"; and *iki kata* (ee-kee kah-tah), or "way of living."

There are dozens of other kata. In fact, there is hardly an area of Japanese thought or behavior that is not directly influenced by one or more kata.

When used in the Japanese context, the shikata concept includes more than just the mechanical process of doing something. It also incorporates the physical and spiritual laws of the cosmos. It refers to the way things are supposed to be done, both the form and the order, as a means of expressing and maintaining harmony in society and the universe.

The absence of shikata is virtually unthinkable to the Japanese, for that refers to an unreal world without order or form. On an everyday level, when the Japanese are faced with something that cannot be changed or controlled (or for some reason they don't want to make the necessary effort) they say, *Shikata ga nai* ("There is no way")—meaning it is utterly hopeless and therefore makes no sense to even try.

Early in their history, the Japanese developed the belief that form had a reality of its own, and that it took precedence over

The absence of *shikata* is unthinkable to the Japanese, as it refers to a world without form/order. When faced with something that can't be controlled, they say *shikata ga nai*—meaning it is hopeless and thus makes no sense to try.

substance. They also believed that anything could be accomplished if the right kata was mentally and physically practiced long enough.

"Japan has no genuine philosophy as such, only form," says Kazuo Matsumura, assistant professor of Japanese mythology at the Oyasato Institute at Tenri University in Nara. He adds, however, that most Japanese today are ignorant of the roots of much of their kata-ized behavior.

The sum total of all the kata in Japanese life has traditionally been referred to as "The Japanese Way." It was the existence of this very conspicuous "way" that provided the Japanese with some of their most enviable attributes—as well as their most negative—and distinguished them from other nationalities.

Most of Japan's numerous kata have been well established for centuries. Over the generations, the kata not only became institutionalized; they also became ritualized and sanctified. Doing things the right way was often more important than doing the right things!

Eventually, the proper observance of kata was equated with morality. One was either "in" kata—*kata ni hamaru* (kah-tah nee hah-mah-rue)—or "out" of kata—*kata ni hamaranai* (kah-tah nee hah-mah-rah-nigh). Being "out of kata" was a sin against society, and even fatal in form-conscious Japan.

Ethics gave way to styles; principles gave way to policies. Just as there was only one acceptable way to perform all the various actions of life in pre-industrial Japan, from using chopsticks to wrapping a package, there was naturally only one right way of thinking—the "Japanese" way.

Cultural conditioning based on the kata system made the Japanese extremely sensitive to any thought, manner, or action that did not conform perfectly to the appropriate kata. In formal, as well as many daily situations, every action was right or wrong, natural or unnatural. There were no shades of gray that accommodated individualistic thought, preferences, or personal idiosyncrasies.

To the Japanese, there was an inner order (the individual heart) and a natural order (the cosmos), and these two were linked together by form—by kata. It was kata that linked the individual and society. If one did not follow the correct form, he was out of harmony with both his fellow man and nature. The challenge facing the Japanese was to know their own *honshin* (hone-sheen), "true" or "right heart," then learn and follow the kata that would keep them in sync with society and the cosmos.

Mental Training

Since the 13th century, yen priests have been teaching the Japanese that mental training is just as important, if not more so, than physical training when it comes to the achieving of harmony and the mastery of any skill.

For young men in feudal Japan's samurai families, this early mental teaching combined aesthetics with the more mundane skills of the world, particularly sword-fighting, which was frequently the final test in one's education—the inept pupil sometimes forfeiting his life.

The ultimate goal in traditional Japanese education among the samurai and professional classes was for the pupil to become one with the object of his training. The goal of the swordsman was to merge his consciousness with his sword; the painter with his brush; the potter with his clay; the garden designer with the materials of the garden. Once this was achieved, as the theory goes, the doing of a thing perfectly was as easy as thinking it.

Over the centuries, each skill and profession making up the Japanese way of living was reduced to its basic elements. The elements were identified and labeled according to their order and the role they played in making up the whole.

The learning of everyday behavior, proper etiquette, work skills, and professions became a codified process of first learning the basic parts and then developing skill in accomplishing the necessary actions in the prescribed order and manner.

Lifelong conditioning in this intricate, finely meshed web of rules and forms made it second nature for the Japanese to expect that every situation would have its exact process and form. When they were confronted with a situation that did not have its own kata, they were either incapable of action, or they took action, sometimes violent, that was often the opposite of common sense.

The significant difference between the Japanese Way and the customs that developed in most other societies was that the Japanese kata-ized their whole existence. Practically nothing was left to chance or personal inclinations. The kata factor was applied to everything, down to the arrangement of food on a tray.

In addition, the Japanese goal was not just the minimum acceptable standard of behavior, action or work. The goal was absolute perfection.

While few Japanese actually achieved total perfection in their behavior or pursuits, a very large percentage of the population certainly achieved a level of competence in the culture that starkly distinguished them from other national groups.

And, as was graphically demonstrated in the latter half of the 20th century, the desire for total perfection in their pursuits ultimately gave them a number of real advantages in competing with the outside world.

The Shikata of Harmony

The hallmark of Japan's kata-ized culture from earliest times has been the promotion and maintenance of *wa* (wah), or harmony. Personal behavior, as well as all private and public relationships, was based on strictly controlled harmony in the proper inferior–superior context of Japanese society.

This religious striving for harmony often went to the extreme and resulted in the creation of many laws and customs that could be considered inhuman, such as collective guilt when only a single individual was at fault.

Part of the rationale for this fascinating system can be traced to the political policies espoused by Prince Shotoku, who served as regent to Empress Suiko in the 7th century. Shotoku was responsible for codifying the idealized virtues of the Japanese in the country's first "constitution."

Prince Shotoku's constitution consisted of seventeen articles that provided the framework within which the country's unique culture was to develop thereafter. The first of these articles made harmony the foundation for all of the others.

Prince Shotoku said that harmony consisted of not making polarized distinctions, and added that if a distinction could be made between good and bad, then harmony did not exist.

The prince was also well aware that envy can destroy harmony. In another article, he proclaimed, "If we envy other men, other men will envy us too. Evil derived from envy knows no end; thus people tend not to rejoice in superior wisdom. If you have superior talent you will be the object of envy."

The constitution's final article was: "You must never decide great matters on your own. You must always discuss them with all kinds of people."

This effort to eliminate envy, prohibit individualism and suppress talent became a vital theme in Japanese culture. The late Shoichi Watanabe, who was a linguist and historian at Jochi (Sophia) University, characterized the government policy of the Edo/Tokugawa period (1603–1868) as "eschew envy; hate ability; revere the past."

During the Edo period, the shogunate passed numerous laws that prevented the development of commerce, the spread of new ideas, and any rise in the standard of living. It was all in an effort to prevent changes in lifestyles and the appearance of such factors as envy and individual competition.

One of the Edo shoguns decreed: "You must never invent anything new!"

Professor Watanabe advanced the theory that the best way to discern and describe the traditional wa-oriented character of the Japanese is to compare them to peasant-farmers, locked in time and place, on a finite piece of soil from which they gain their livelihood. He said that a key part of the mentality that developed from this intimate relationship with land was a compulsion for harmony, since the survival of each village literally depended upon the strict observance of mutual concern and cooperation to build and maintain the complex irrigation systems needed to grow rice.

This "village mentality" prevails in Japan to this day in the form of groups and factions in business, politics, education and elsewhere. The Japanese still tend to regard any threat to the harmony of their immediate group, to their company or their country, as a matter of life and death, and to do whatever is necessary to protect and maintain wa.

Professor Watanabe also concluded that the respect for harmony is so strong in Japan that it continues to weed out most of the more competent, maverick-type individuals, frequently resulting in inferior leaders reaching the summit of the seniority system in all areas of Japanese life.

Amae refers a kind of love ideally found between infant and mother. The infant utterly relies on the mother to do what is right and best for it.

Examples of this syndrome are so commonplace in Japan that they are ordinarily taken for granted. Exceptions are growing, however, particularly in the political arena, where efforts to find and place acceptable prime ministers and other top officials have degenerated into a farce that the news media and people at large no longer accept without question.

A key factor in the Japanese culture of harmony is an attitude described by the word *amae* (ah-my-eh), which means something like "indulgent love," and is the kind of love ideally found between infant and mother. The infant is utterly dependent on the mother and must totally trust the mother to do what is right and best for it. Likewise, the infant can indulge in the mother's forgiveness even when it is behaving badly.

Unquestioned "indulgent love" is, of course, known outside of Japan, but in the West its application is generally limited to infants and very young children. In Japan, however, it became one of the foundations for all relationships throughout life.

Traditional Japanese society incorporated the *amae* concept within specifically categorized and defined life-roles called *bun* (boon), which determined obligations and lifestyle within the individual categories. There was a *bun*—and *kata*—for carpenters, for merchants, for samurai, for students, and even for professional gangsters.

These life-role *bun* provided strict guidelines for the prescribed relationship between children and parents, between younger and older siblings, between workers and their superiors, between samurai warriors and their lords, between the nation as a whole and the emperor.

All of these relationships in turn had their own kata-ized behavioral guides. The proper functioning of *bun* was based on every person knowing his place in life and keeping it according to the prescribed form, all the while demonstrating honesty, integrity, goodwill, trust, confidence and selflessness.

Of course, the system seldom functioned fully, but the mass effort of the Japanese to live up to the expectations of their own kata-ized *bun* was one of the primary factors that shaped their character—and contributed to some early foreign residents remarking that living in Japan was like being in a kind of well-ordered paradise.

There were also other cultural factors designed to encourage or compel the Japanese to follow the kata-ized modes of behavior required by the *bun* roles of each individual. The most important of these concepts was expressed in the term *giri* (ghee-ree), which means "obligations." There were specific obligations that each person had to others—to teachers, employers, lords, and so on.

These obligations were spelled out in detail, and failure to fulfill them was a serious matter. Ostracism and banishment were some of the lighter punishments for the worst transgressions.

The immediate social sanction used to enforce strict obedience to the life obligations of the Japanese was shame, which was sometimes so intense and overpowering that the only acceptable recourse was suicide.

義理. Meaning: duty. Kana reading: ぎり. Romaji reading (pronunciation): *giri*.

義
理

One of the results of this system was that the Japanese became intensely sensitive to the threat of shame, suspicious of the motives of others, and correspondingly conditioned to seek revenge when they felt they had been wronged.

Both *giri* and shame are still very much alive in present-day Japan. One also constantly hears references to obligations that someone must fulfill because of his role in life—often much to his chagrin. These include obligatory gifts, attendance at weddings and funerals, catering to superiors, etc.

Taking revenge, usually in subtle, behind-the-scene ways, remains a common preoccupation. Japanese still strive to put and keep all of their relationships, personal as well as business, on an *amae*-impregnated role/rank basis. This is the factor that is at play when they go to such lengths and put so much stock in developing close, intimate relationships with foreigners before doing business with them.

Most Japanese are unable to feel comfortable in anything but a clearly defined socially ranked relationship "made safe" by the belief that they can expect indulgence from the other party when accidentally or purposely breaking some of the rules of the relationship.

Many Japanese, in all areas of business and government, attribute the country's Phoenix-like recovery from the destruction of World War II to the principle of kata-ized *wa* that underpins their culture. They hold that it was harmonious relations between labor and management, between business and the government and between individuals that made it possible for the people to work together with a single-minded determination that created the so-called economic miracle.

Other commentators, particularly long-term foreign residents who have become bilingual and bicultural, say that the still-powerful shame syndrome and a consuming pride were the primary motivating factors that drove the Japanese in their superhuman efforts to not only rebuild their country, but to become one of the world's leading economic powers.

Social harmony, based on following proper etiquette kata in daily behavior (under the threat of being ostracized), remains

Japanese calligraphy, the word "peace" and the signature of the calligrapher, Baron Ōura Kanetake, 1910.

the guiding principle in all Japanese relations, whether personal, business or political.

Wa pervades the culture. It appears as wall art in the form of calligraphy. It is a key part of such common words as peace *(heiwa)*, peaceful resolution *(wa kai)*, and peaceful concord *(wa go)*. The original name of the country, Yamato, is written with the characters for "Great Harmony" *(Dai Wa)*.

The deeply entrenched concept of "Japanese Spirit," Yamato Damashii, can be read as *wa kon* when the character for "great" is dropped.

Some Japanese who attribute the country's success to the spirit of wa claim it is contained in their genes. This, of course, is nonsense, as is evidenced by the Japanese-Americans who are fully assimilated into American culture and, as American expatriate businessman Joe Schmelzeis Jr. says, "speak with their mouths, not their bellies." Japan marketing guru George Fields also disagrees with this theory. He says wa in Japan today is better described in business terms, as "corporate spirit, unity of employees, and the consumer always comes last." He adds that much of the wa that survives in Japan results from government pressure and guidance.

Examples of Japanese-style wa abound. Candid government officials and company executives used to readily admit back in the 1980s that *dango* (dahn-go), or "bid rigging," was common in Japan, but to them it is just wa at work. Until foreigners began complaining about the practice, it was not considered an ethical issue. The Japanese involved were perplexed and irritated that foreigners made an issue of it, but a few isolated complaints from outsiders are not enough to eliminate a culturally entrenched kata that serves the Japanese establishment so well.

The original goal of wa was social harmony and political control. Now, as George Fields notes, its primary role is to contribute to economic success on corporate, industrial, and national levels.

In practice, the Japanese government's policy of promoting harmony sometimes clashes with the interests of individual companies, and corporate managers go along with it grudgingly. On a company level, adherence to the principles of wa is usually confined to the company itself and to any closely affiliated companies. Sub-contract firms are generally treated as expendable. Other outside firms are regarded as competitors and adversaries.

A not surprising characteristic of the Japanese that derives from their emphasis on correct form and harmony is their tendency to avoid doing things together if they are uncertain about how to do them. This trait is part of the reason the Japanese are often reluctant to set any precedent and habitually wait for someone else or some other company to take the lead. This attitude is often one of the main barriers foreign companies face in attempting to do business in Japan.

The Feeling of Rightness

Born and raised in a cultural environment that was the result of centuries of conditioning in the art of living Japanese style and in the use of arts and crafts that were products of rigidly controlled kata, each Japanese naturally developed a sixth sense that told him or her when things were "right"—that is, when they were designed, made, assembled, packaged, or whatever in accordance with Japanese concepts of aesthetics, appropriate materials, form, feel, purpose, and method of use.

Over the centuries these standards became higher and higher, ultimately demanding that even the most commonplace product be a masterpiece of craftsmanship and all service be performed with consummate, stylized skill. Japanese naturally became so sensitive to the rightness or correctness of any service or product, measured by absolute Japanese standards, that they knew almost instinctively when something did not measure up to these standards. This traditional characteristic reaction made them among the most discriminating people in the world, and often the quickest to pass judgment.

Japan's modern-day reputation for cheap, shoddy products, which endured from 1870 until the 1960s, was not of their own doing, and undeserved. When the country was opened to the West in the 1860s, foreign importers flocked in, bringing with them samples of Western products they wanted copied at the lowest possible prices.

These first foreign importers and those who followed them determined the quality of most of Japan's exports until the Japanese became strong enough to escape from their influence nearly one hundred years later.

While social and economic changes in Japan have greatly diluted kata-ized conditioning in the traditional culture and, subsequently, the discriminating abilities of Japanese born after 1945, the Japanese as a group are still among the most critical people in the world. Their culturally produced emphasis on aesthetic excellence, quality and propriety remains one of their primary strengths. It gives them an edge in designing, manufacturing and packaging products, as well as in promoting and selling them. It also makes them very demanding customers.

This aspect of modern Japanese culture is so prominent that Japanologist-linguist Ken Butler says that generally, the Japanese are innately imbued with the attitudes and skills that make good businessmen.

The Uniqueness Factor

Long centuries of living within the kata-ized Japanese way and never seeing, much less experiencing, any other way of daily life naturally led the Japanese to become acutely sensitive to any deviation from their way of doing things. This factor contributed significantly to their developing especially strong feelings of being unique in the world—feelings that persist today and influence their personal behavior toward non-Japanese, business relations with foreign companies, and government policy in international affairs.

These differences are so conspicuous that one veteran observer, paraphrasing an earlier commentator, said jokingly: "The Japanese are so unique that it is uniquely impossible to describe their uniqueness."

Unfortunately, Japanese feelings of uniqueness are often expressed in a very negative manner. Among other things, it makes it very difficult, or impossible, for un-Westernized Japanese to relate to non-Japanese. Even other Japanese who become partially de-Japanized by spending time abroad are treated, in varying degrees, as outcasts in their own society after they return home.

School children who have spent time abroad and lost some of their Japaneseness are harassed by other students and in many cases even their teachers. (In recent decades, special schools have been built to help re-acculturate such children so that they are better able to re-enter Japanese society.)

Businessmen who have picked up foreign attitudes and mannerisms while serving their companies on overseas assignments often find that they are no longer fully accepted by their own co-workers or management when they return home. Until the

1990s most major Japanese companies tended to follow a policy of not hiring non-Japanese employees within Japan, including ethnic Korean and Chinese residents who were born and raised in Japan, are citizens and are virtually indistinguishable from ethnic Japanese.

The rationale for this policy was that non-Japanese do not, and cannot, fit into the Japanese system because they are not Japanese. This discrimination has also been applied to Japan's minority population of "untouchables," whose only difference is that they are descendants of Japanese who were involved in the slaughter of animals and working with animal hides during the country's Buddhist-dominated period.

Until recent decades, larger Japanese firms were known to have bought lists of names and addresses of families in this group in order to avoid inadvertently hiring one...there being no other way to distinguish them from other Japanese.

Japanese feelings of uniqueness are frequently taken to even further extremes, making them appear foolish. Attempting to justify import barriers against foreign-made ski equipment by claiming that snow in Japan is different from snow in other countries (so the equipment won't work in Japan) is just one example. (The fact that they were exporting Japanese-made skis did not have any effect on the reasoning of the trade associations involved.)

In the past, Japanese have also used their perceived uniqueness to justify all kinds of discrimination against both foreign nationals and products at every level of Japanese society, an attitude once part of their national policy. This attitude and behavior were directly opposed to attempts to bring the economy into the global fold, and thwarted many of the efforts on both the government and private levels.

Racial, cultural, sexual and age discrimination by Japanese companies is not limited to their domestic practices. Some take the same mind-set with them overseas, where they have encountered serious repercussions from their refusal to hire blacks and sometimes whites as well.

Kata Comes First

The Japanese were traditionally conditioned to get their pleasure from conforming to kata, from doing things in the prescribed manner. One of the effects of this conditioning was to make the Japanese process-oriented instead of result-oriented. Westerners are fond of saying, "I don't care how you do it, just get it done." Japanese tend to say, "Don't do it unless you can do it right (the right way)."

Japanese are happiest when they improve on a process, says management guru Masaru Chio. "They are perfectionists. The slightest flaw in anything attracts their attention and they cannot rest until it is eliminated," he adds. Because of this attitude there is a strong tendency for the Japanese to try to improve on any job they undertake, particularly when using technology or copying products imported from abroad.

They often seem to spend as much or more time on refining processes as they do on producing results. But once refinements have been made, their performance often shoots upward.

Not surprisingly, the traditional Japanese standard when measuring or evaluating individuals is attitude first, effort second, and results third. In sports and other activities, participants are honored and rewarded in recognition of their attitude, spirit and effort as well as their victories.

Proper observance of every traditional kata in today's Japan is no longer a life-and-death issue, and some kata have nearly disappeared. However, others are still of vital importance, coloring and often controlling the thoughts and actions of virtually all adult Japanese in many areas of their lives.

Japanese kata for negotiating, for example, play a vital role not only in business, but in international relations as well. Kinhide Mushakoji, formerly professor of international relations at Jochi (Sophia) University in Tokyo, described the Japanese kata of diplomacy and negotiating as the art of *awase* (ah-wah-say), or "adjustment," while Westerners follow an *erabi* (eh-rah-bee), or "choice" style.

In other words, the Japanese negotiate by adjusting or adapting to differences, while Westerners negotiate by selecting specific options. The Japanese take a broad, flexible approach. Westerners tend to take a more narrow, highly defined approach. The Japanese seek nonspecific generalities that take into account all the shades in between specifics. Westerners demand a logical structure made up of specific concepts and their opposites.

Japanese society lives by the kata of adjustment, seemingly with few hard and fast ethics or clear-cut moral rules of the type found in Western cultures. It is soft and flexible and can be readily manipulated by self-seeking and aggressive individuals and groups within the society.

Christianized societies, on the other hand, attempt to live by principles embodying hard, inflexible rules. It should not be surprising that meetings between Japanese and Westerners often result in misunderstandings and friction.

The Coming of Foreigners

Because of the intense cultural conditioning undergone by all Japanese during the feudal age, any deviation from "correct" thought and form was a serious moral and ethical transgression. Behaving in any way other than "the Japanese way" was unthinkable for the average person.

Thus, when foreigners who behaved in a vastly different manner began showing up in Japan the Japanese were shocked at their lack of kata and crude etiquette. To the Japanese the foreigners looked, behaved and smelled like "hairy barbarians" with whom they had almost nothing in common.

Still, today the Japanese are extraordinarily sensitive to the appearance, attitudes, and behavior of foreigners. Because of the exclusivity of Japanese culture, the Japanese are unable to accept foreigners as equals, and tend to be comfortable with them only when they are in Japan as temporary visitors. As long as foreigners can be treated as guests, the Japanese are able to exempt them from the demands of Japanese culture, and can extend extraordinary courtesies and privileges to them.

Non-guest foreigners inevitably encounter the cultural dichotomy that prevents the Japanese from fully accepting them on any basis except as temporary visitors. Foreigners in Japan must therefore continuously be aware that as tolerant and hospitable as their Japanese hosts are to short-term visitors, who are not expected to know or practice their kata-ized etiquette, they are still emotionally affected when anyone, foreigners included, behaves "incorrectly."

Over and above this sensitivity, the Japanese are prone to regard normal "give-and-take" Western behavior as arrogant, often inhuman and typically ill-mannered, while Japanese behavior often appears insincere, devious and dishonest to Westerners once they get beyond the famous facade of Japanese courtesy.

Intimate knowledge of the kata factor helps to bridge this cultural chasm by sensitizing the "visiting" foreigner to the need to observe "proper" behavior, and to avoid situations in which non-conformity would seriously jeopardize the goals at hand.

It is especially important for foreign businessmen, politicians and diplomats dealing with the Japanese to become familiar with Japan's kata-ized etiquette system and their special sensitivities in order to avoid creating unnecessary ill will.

Specific kata and how they impact on all inter-personal relationships with the Japanese, along with strategies for dealing with them, are discussed in some detail in the following chapters.

2

The Kata-ization of Japan

The Way of the Gods

THE origins of Japan's kata can be traced back to a number of historical influences, beginning with the native religion of Shintoism, translated as "The Way of the Gods," as well as the introduction of the irrigation method of rice farming, and the importation of Buddhism, Confucianism, the ideographic writing system, and various other cultural artifacts from China.

Shintoism is an animistic belief based on cosmic harmony among gods, spirits, people, and the physical world of nature. It is the indirect, but culturally pervasive, source of many of the attitudes and customs that distinguish the Japanese from all other people. It was apparently the influence of Shintoism that led the Japanese to refer to themselves as the people of Wa, attesting to a very early commitment by the Japanese to the principle of harmony as the foundation for their society.

The first emperors of Japan combined the functions of religious and secular leaders, serving as high priests as well as sovereigns. The emperors and their courts were thus as much concerned with form as with essence. An over-riding principle, adopted from Confucianism, was harmony between heaven and earth, and between rulers and the ruled.

This led to the development of a highly controlled behavior designed to express subservience and respect toward superior beings. The stylized ceremonies associated with worship were thus infused into the conduct of daily affairs.

The Japanese affinity for formalizing, institutionalizing, and ritualizing procedures and processes may not have actually originated in Shintoism, but this characteristic Japanese behavior was surely nurtured by the pervasive religious practices that marked life in early Japan.

Conducting precise religious rituals dozens of times through-out each year was a major aspect of Japanese life from the dawn of their history, and in each family at least one member was expected to be versed in these rites.

Whatever the origin of the wa concept, it was to become one of the main threads in the cultural fabric of Japan, influencing its form, its texture, its color, and its spirit.

The Way of Wet-rice Farming

Japanese social anthropologists believe that the introduction of irrigated wet-rice farming into Japan from China, sometime between 1,000 and 300 B.C., had an especially profound effect on the country's social system and subsequently the character and behavior of the Japanese.[1]

Many historians claim that the lifestyle that emerged with wet-rice farming in such a limited land area imbued the Japanese with an extraordinary degree of patience, perseverance, diligence, cooperativeness, and group dependence because this kind of farming required very elaborate irrigation systems that could not easily be built and maintained—or protected from marauders—by single families.

---

[1] Although the life-styles of the great mass of Chinese peasantry had long since been kata-ized, imbuing them with many similar cultural traits that were later to become characteristic of the Japanese, the Chinese were then and are still now significantly different from the Japanese. China is physically huge. There are immense differences in the terrain and the climate. The country is equally diverse ethnically and culturally, with dozens of languages. Throughout the history of the country, distance and politics limited cultural progress and homogenization to a tiny percentage of the popula-tion. Continued political oppression and lack of personal freedom have kept many Chinese—still today—from being able to fully realize their enormous Japanese-type potential.

At the Hakone Shrine in Hakone, Japan, a bright red/orange *torii* gate marks the transition from the mortal world to the realm of the sacred and divine.

Among the most conspicuous Japanese traits said to have been fostered by wet-rice farming was the acceptance of discipline and regimentation. The individual who did not conform was quickly ostracized to protect and sustain the group. The process of rice farming was prescribed down to the last detail. Any deviation angered not only one's family, friends and neighbors, but the gods as well. The whole economic base of the country therefore became one giant rice-raising kata that made group behavior, cooperation, self-sacrifice and harmony mandatory.

Also very early in Japan's history, probably sometime before A.D. 300, the concept of *kochi komin* (koe-chee koe-meen), in which the land and the people belonged to the emperor and the people had no ultimate right to own private property or to be independent, was imported from China.

This helped to set the stage for absolute control of the people by the state and the development of many of the other cultural traits that were to distinguish the Japanese in modern times.

The Country of Wa

Prior to A.D. 300, Japanese society consisted of relatively independent family clans that exercised domain in their own small areas. Around A.D. 300, one of these clans became paramount in the area now known as Nara Prefecture (a short distance from Kyoto and Osaka) and established itself as the Yamato Court, claiming sovereignty over the entire country. Later historians labeled the first leader of the Yamato Court as Jimmu *Tenno*, or Emperor Jimmu.

Later emperors continued the process of unifying the country, which came to be known as *Yamato* (Yah-mah-toh) after the founding clan. Yamato is another reading for the word wa, or

Farmer working in a rice field. The introduction of wet-rice farming from China to Japan is believed to have imbued the Japanese with diligence, patience, cooperativeness, and perseverance in order to combat the difficult labor.

harmony, once again attesting to an early fundamental commitment by the Japanese to the concept of a harmonious society.

Following the ascendancy of Japan's Yamato Court to power, however, several military expeditions were launched against Korea—an early sign that harmony in the Japanese context was primarily designed to shape and channel Japanese behavior for internal purposes and did not specifically apply to their relationships with outsiders.

These Japanese raids on Korea resulted in a mass influx of Chinese-Korean cultural influences into Japan, mostly through Korean prisoners and immigrants, and later Chinese scholars and priests. Thereafter, Korea and China were to play leading roles in the development of both culture and kata in Japan.

From around A.D. 550, two-way travel and trade between Japan, Korea, and China became quite common. Religious scholars in particular served as conduits for importing Chinese culture into the islands. The ritualized ceremonies of China's Imperial Court, as well as the sophisticated etiquette that China's ministers and mandarins had developed over a period of more than 3,000 years, were gradually assimilated into Japan's already highly structured Imperial system.

Decorum and language appropriate for addressing the godlike emperor of Japan became exquisitely stylized and ultimately codified. Every movement of the body, every stance, even the tone of the voice, was precisely established. An only slightly less lofty level of etiquette was required for other members of the Imperial Court.

As time passed, a system of clan fiefs and clan lords became the paramount political and social structure in Japan. These clan lords set up their own governments, patterning them after the Imperial Court in form as well as ritualistic behavior. Court etiquette was thus brought to elite families throughout the country, further strengthening the custom of ritualizing all training and learning.

The Mother Kata

When Japan first began interactions with Korea and China, the Japanese had no system of writing. Around the middle of the 3rd century, a scholar named Wani brought from Korea to Japan several volumes of the Analects of Confucius and a textbook for studying the Chinese writing system, but very little came of this incident.

By the early 4th century, however, the Imperial Court of Japan was employing Koreans who had migrated to Japan to serve as official recorders using the Chinese way of writing, which the Japanese called *Kanji* (Kahn-jee), or "Chinese letters."

Kanji had gradually evolved in China over a period of a thousand years or so, beginning as rather straightforward "pictures" of the things and ideas they represented. Little by little, these pictures were stylized to make them more consistent in shape and size, and therefore easier to draw in large numbers on small sheets or scrolls of paper, as well as more aesthetically attractive. By the time the "characters" arrived in Japan, they were the world's most sophisticated writing system.

Over the next hundred or so years, the descendants of these Korean scribes gradually transcribed most of the Japanese language into Kanji. In this extraordinary grafting process, they used the Japanese pronunciation when the original meaning of the Chinese ideograms and the Japanese words were the same, and maintained the Chinese pronunciation when they were not.

Since each Chinese character expressed a single idea, it was necessary to make numerous adaptations and additions to the system in order to express complete thoughts in Japanese. An example of one of these adaptations was to use Chinese characters that had the same sound as Japanese syllables or words, regardless of the original meaning of the Chinese ideograms. Another method was to use a phonetic script to add the proper Japanese-word endings to the base Chinese characters.

Memorizing and learning how to read and write thousands of complicated Chinese characters, with their multiple pronunciations, was a challenge of immense proportions and beyond the means of most Japanese who lacked the time and motivation.

In keeping with Confucian principles of separating the sexes, females were forbidden to study the imported Chinese ideograms. Because of this Imperial edict, ladies of the Imperial Court and the aristocracy resorted to using the word-ending phonetic script, and subsequently played a key role in developing it into a simple shorthand system of writing the entire language phonetically.

This new phonetic syllabic system developed by upper-class women became known as *onna-te* (own-nah tay), or "women's hand," since it was used almost exclusively by women for private communication and the writing of poetry, diaries, and novels. This is the writing system now known as *hiragana* (hee-rah-gah-nah), or "flat letters."

In a further effort to simplify the writing of the language, a totally separate phonetic system, derived from parts of the multi-stroke Chinese characters, was developed by scholars in the 9th and 10th centuries. This second phonetic system became known as *katakana* (kah-tah-kah-nah), or "incomplete letters." This system is the one now used in Japan for writing the thousands of foreign words that have been absorbed into the language.

Despite the creation of two phonetic writing systems, the difficult Kanji remained a part of the writing system of the Imperial Court, the agencies of the government, the priesthood, and the male members of the upper classes for centuries, eventually becoming one of the primary crucibles of Japanese culture and the Japanese that we know today.

Each Kanji was made up of one to a dozen or more conjoining strokes. The order in which each stroke was to be executed was carefully prescribed, and no deviation was allowed. Among Japan's upper class, boys began the long process of learning how to read and write Kanji from about the age of five, spending a number of hours each day for the next several years practicing the prescribed kaki-kata, or "way of writing."

Since the Chinese ideographs depicted actual things and concepts, they communicated more than just sounds as per our familiar ABCs. Using Kanji as a system of communicating and recording information and concepts was therefore much more of a personal experience, with far deeper and stronger psychological content than words spelled with phonetic letters.

In a recent experiment where various strokes were combined to create non-existent Kanji, Japanese respondents frequently argued with each other over the "correct" meanings of the "characters." The mental focus and kata-ized mechanical effort required to memorize and write thousands of Kanji in a correct manner had a fundamental affect on the psychological and physical development of all educated Japanese males. It ingrained in them patience and diligence, enhanced manual dexterity well beyond the norm, and prepared them for a lifestyle in which form and order were paramount.

Learning how to draw the Kanji characters also imbued the educated Japanese with a highly developed sense of harmony, form, and style that combined to give them a deep understanding and appreciation of aesthetics, making each of them an artist of no little skill.

In addition to making the Japanese good at doing small, complicated things with their hands and enhancing their sensitivity to forms and designs, training in writing Kanji also conditioned the Japanese to be patient and to persevere in their goals. The long-term practice of Kanji thus became a mold that shaped the Japanese physically, emotionally, and intellectually, homogenizing them and binding them to their culture.

Learning Kanji during Japan's long feudal age did not end with mastering their pronunciations, meanings and correct stroke order. Every student of the art was also required to become adept at drawing the characters in a stylized manner known as *Shodo* (show-doh), or "The Way of the Brush," or simply calligraphy in English.

When skill in writing the Kanji ideograms was pursued beyond basic requirements, which many Japanese did, it became a fine art. The greatest calligraphers won lasting fame. In fact, skill in writing the ideograms became so important during the heyday of Japan's feudal age (A.D. 1192–1868) that how well one wrote became a measure of his character and worthiness.

Midway during the period that the character and skill building Kanji writing system was being introduced into Japan, the Imperial government institutionalized the concept of a carefully prescribed harmony. *Wa* (harmony) became the official policy of the government in A.D. 604, when Prince Shotoku named it as the foundation of all human relations in his famous "Seventeen Articles," which historians were to call Japan's first constitution later on.

With wa firmly established as the essence of their social system, the upper-class Japanese thereafter fashioned all their social rules and institutions, as well as their language, to contribute to the cultural goal of harmony. No area or facet of Japanese life was untouched by this one overriding principle.

Handicrafts and Art

Along with the Chinese writing system, the Japanese of this early age also imported virtually all the leading Chinese arts and crafts, along with the master–apprentice teaching system, creating new cottage industries that eventually spread throughout the country. Once the Japanese learned the basics of these new arts and crafts, they began experimenting with the designs and production techniques, adapting them to suit their own tastes.

Learning the skills necessary to duplicate a Chinese handicraft or fine art took many years, however, and sometimes more than one lifetime. Boys, often as young as eight or nine, were apprenticed to skilled craftsmen and artists, sometimes for as many as thirty or even forty years, to master each craft or art. They in turn passed the skill on to their own apprentices.

Given their natural propensity for structuring and formalizing everything, the earliest of these Japanese craftsmen and artists refined their specialized techniques into minutely detailed kata that covered not only physical actions but attitudes as well.

Every thought, every move, every nuance of the kata of the arts and crafts were established, and—just as in writing Kanji—deviations were not tolerated.

While this ensured that the mastery of each craft would be passed on from generation to generation, in many cases it also prevented further experimentation and change—a factor that was eventually to contribute to the stagnation of Japanese culture during the final centuries of the feudal era.

In one sense, the Japanese of feudal Japan were in training for nearly two thousand years for the opportunities that were to be presented to them in 1945, when for the first time in their history, they gained much broader individual freedom and could engage freely in a more unrestrained and competitive market.

It was only in such a free environment that they could fully utilize the distinct sensibilities and skills they had developed over a period of nearly two millennia.

Shikata of the Samurai

By the beginning of the 12th century, most of the authority of Japan's Imperial Court had been usurped by powerful provincial clan lords who maintained their own armies of warriors. In the 1180s, Yoritomo Minamoto, a leader of one of these warrior groups, defeated the other lords in a series of battles and emerged as the supreme power in the country.

Minamoto petitioned the reigning emperor for approval to set up a military government to administer the civil and military affairs of the country, and to use the title *Shogun* (Show-goon), or Generalissimo.[2] The emperor had little choice.

Minamoto established his headquarters in Kamakura, far to the northeast of the Imperial capital of Kyoto (a one-hour

[2] Shogun is short for Sei-i-tai Shogun (Say-e-e-tie Show-goon) or Barbarian Subduing Generalissimo, used centuries earlier in campaigns against the indigenous Ainu people who inhabited the northern regions of Japan when the racial groups which came to be known as the Japanese arrived on the scene.

train-ride south of present-day Tokyo). He then confirmed the positions of the provincial clan lords who had fought on his side during the war and confiscated the lands of the losing lords, reassigning them to his allies.

The Kamakura period marked the beginning of the shogunate system of military government that was to prevail in Japan until 1868, nearly 700 years later, when the last shogun stepped down.

Warriors of the shogunate and the clan lords were known as samurai, a derivative of the word meaning "to guard" or "guards." The profession of samurai soon became hereditary and reached new levels of development as a class of warrior families ranked at the top of the social system.

Over the generations, the samurai warriors developed their own "class" kata comprising a collective code of thought and conduct known as *Bushido* (Boo-she-doe), or "The Way of the Warrior," which applied to all the members of their families.

This code demanded absolute loyalty to the clan lord, extraordinary skill with the sword and other weapons of war on the part of male members of samurai families, and adherence to the ritualized etiquette followed by the Imperial and clan courts.

Bushido required supreme dedication and effort. The discipline and techniques of Zen Buddhism, which was introduced into Japan from China during the 13th century, were quickly adopted by the samurai and became one of the primary vehicles for their physical as well as spiritual training.

Zen was a significant move away from the mystical and esoteric beliefs and practices of Shintoism and Buddhism. It was based on realism and practicality. Its goal was to help advocates discern between the real and the imaginary, and to achieve perfect harmony between the body and the mind through rigorous mental and physical discipline.

The goal of Zen followers in feudal Japan was to make all of the actions of life an expression of Zen-actions that could be per-

The armor of an ancient samurai. In ancient Japan, the *bushido* code demanded, above all else, absolute loyalty to the clan lord.

fected only through meditation to achieve harmony with the universe, followed by physical practice to teach the body the proper moves. Every adherent was to be an example of living Zen.

Zen practice was just as carefully codified as the making of a piece of pottery or proper behavior in greeting and conversing with a high-ranking superior. There was a prescribed way for the process from beginning to end. Meditation was the way to understanding the relationship between man and the world at large. Mental discipline was the key to controlling and directing the body. Endless physical practice in the desired skills was the third step in Zen training.

Training in Zen practices was ritualized, institutionalized, and kata-ized like everything else in Japanese life. Zen priests were also hard taskmasters, demanding extraordinary endurance, perseverance and dedication from those wanting to sharpen their mental and physical skills as well as their awareness. Those who rigorously pursued Zen practices for many years often developed a kind of sixth sense that greatly expanded their ability to hear and understand and to "know" things that could not be seen.

The Zen-inspired kata training system of the samurai also further conditioned this elite class of Japanese to sacrifice their lives in the pursuit of perfection and order and the successful execution of their obligations to their masters—all traits that were formerly associated with the Japanese in general.

Japan's many Zen temples are still thriving today and in fact experienced a wave of renewed interest in the 1970s, particularly among business people who rediscovered the advantages of using the traditional discipline and philosophy of Zen as a weapon in their competition with domestic foreign business adversaries.

Between 1970 and 1990, shortly before the popping of the financial bubble, thousands of Japanese managers spent part of their on-the-job training time in Zen temples, undergoing the rigorous discipline of meditation sessions to develop patience, perseverance, endurance and, they hoped, cosmic wisdom.

During the long course of Japan's feudal age when the samurai class reigned supreme (1192–1868), much of the ethics, morality and manners of the samurai were gradually absorbed to a significant degree by the lower classes, particularly by the merchant class that rose during the last centuries of the shogunate dynasties from the mid-17th century and onward.

Shikata of the Swords

The kata of martial arts epitomized the training and lifestyle of the samurai class. Male members of samurai families spent years perfecting their physical and mental skills in the use of the sword. This dedication and training were carried to the point where the sword came to be regarded as semi-sacred and representing the soul, spirit and pride of samurai warriors.

Dropping a samurai's sword or mishandling it in any way brought many luckless Japanese a painful death at the hands of the sword owner.

Sword-making was constantly refined and improved until each weapon was a work of art that surpassed swords made anywhere else in beauty, strength and cutting edge. Swordsmiths would spend months finding the right pieces of metal to blend, then weeks to months working on a single blade.

Fashioning and honing the blade became a Shinto-based ritualistic process intended to imbue the finished sword with its own spirit. The practicing of swordsmanship by all of the males in the samurai class was to have a profound influence on all Japanese and Japanese history from this time on.

Training in the use of the sword began when the sons of samurai were three or four years old, and continued throughout their active lives as warriors. Until the end of the feudalistic shogunate system in 1868, any samurai warrior was legally permitted to cut down, on the spot, any commoner guilty of breaking a law or behaving in a disrespectful manner. This was a great incentive for the Japanese mass to obey all laws and codes of etiquette.

During Japan's long feudal age, only members of the samurai class were allowed to practice swordsmanship, which was known

Japanese short *katana* with sheath. Training with these swords was a serious matters, and this eventually gave rise to training with flexible bamboo strips.

as *Kendo,* or the "Way of the Sword" (usually written in Roman letters as "kendo"). Kendo schools were operated in all the clan fiefs as well as in larger cities and towns.

During the latter feudal centuries, solid wooden staffs were used instead of real swords in the training. Since a stout staff in the hands of a strong opponent can be as deadly as a steel sword, the training and exhibition bouts were very serious matters.

In addition to honing the sword-fighting skills of the samurai, training in kendo also emphasized the spiritual and moral responsibilities of warriors, along with the highly stylized manners that were the hallmark of the samurai class.

Following the establishment of the Tokugawa Shogunate in 1603, and the beginning of a long and peaceful era, the injury and death toll from kendo training became unacceptable. The use of solid staffs ultimately gave way to flexible bamboo strips that were held together by leather fittings. Protective gear that included helmets and facemasks, torso guards, and gauntlets was developed and routinely used except in the case of grudge or revenge bouts when the contestants reverted to the traditional staffs without protection.

When the shogunate system of government and the privileged samurai class were ended in 1868, kendo schools catering to common people soon sprang up. Officers of the Imperial Army of Japan were trained in the use of the sword up to 1945. Following the introduction of democracy into Japan after the end of World War II, the practice of kendo became an important means of developing character rather than martial prowess.

Today, kendo is a popular public school curriculum and is taught in many private kendo schools operated by masters of the art. It is also a significant part of the training of Japanese police.

The kata of kendo, codified hundreds of years ago, is still precisely followed in Japan's kendo schools. All of the moves and thrusts as well as the accompanying etiquette are minutely detailed. Boys begin training as early as the age of five or six. Training sessions are designed to instill courage, aggressiveness, and an inexhaustible spirit—and they do.

Kendo and its kata make a major contribution to the mental and physical training of many Japanese, further conditioning them in the etiquette and morality of the Japanese Way, as well as improving will and spirit in their personal/business dealings.

The Ritual of Tea

Perhaps no aspect of traditional Japanese culture is more representative of the role and importance of kata than the practice of the tea ceremony, or *chanoyu* (chah-no-yuu). The custom of ceremonial tea-drinking was introduced into Japan from Korea and China in the 700s.

At first the custom was followed mainly by emperors, members of the Imperial Court, and Buddhist priests. Priests would gather in front of a statue of Buddha and drink tea with all of the ritualistic formality of a holy sacrament.

As centuries passed, the ceremonial aspects faded, only to be reincorporated during the Kamakura Period (1185–1333). Juko Murata, tea master to Shogun Yoshimasa Ashikaga, is credited with turning the ceremony into an aesthetic ritual in the 1400s.

The ceremony was further developed and codified during the 1500s by the famed Sen no Rikyu. With Shogun Yoshimasa Ashikaga as a patron, the ritualistic drinking of tea quickly developed into a public ceremony that was regularly staged by numerous people. Tea houses abounded.

The ceremony's goal was to develop and demonstrate one's aesthetic abilities and perfectly refined manners. The kata of *chanoyu* was minutely detailed, incorporating not only the place, dress, actions, and state of mind, but also the weather. Staging a ceremony was nothing casual. It required years of practice, and for many was a profession of the most exacting kind. Tea masters were among those honored as the great men of their times.

Practicing *chanoyu* was believed to develop refinement and character along with control of the body and the mind—all traits especially prized by the Japanese.

A public demonstration of a Japanese tea ceremony. The purpose of this event was to demonstrate one's aesthetic abilities and perfectly refined manners.

The tea ceremony remains a major cultural practice in the present day. There are many "schools," hundreds of tea masters, and thousands of specially built rooms where ceremonies are staged regularly. Hundreds of thousands of individuals, particularly successful older men and women, regularly conduct tea ceremonies for special friends as well as just for themselves alone.

In addition to training and exercising aesthetic ability, tea ceremonies also teach Japan's highly refined etiquette, patience, endurance and precision. Practiced properly, a tea ceremony can produce a calming effect on the nerves and emotions, lower one's blood pressure, and even put one in a peaceful mood.

The tea ceremony is not only an exercise in kata culture. It is also a kind of therapy that many Japanese utilize to rid themselves of the stress of the modern-day world, particularly the non-Japanese aspects of present-day society and business.

The Shikata of Sumo

Sumo (sue-moh), or Japanese style wrestling, dates back to far before the beginning of Japan's written history. It is an excellent example of kata because it is in fact a quintessential Japanese activity—demonstrating very publicly the Japanese emphasis on order and form, ceremony and ritual—and because it has survived virtually unchanged and is more popular and significant today than it was a thousand years ago.

Sumo fans are well aware of its detailed kata, from the feeding and training of the wrestlers to their techniques in the ring. Every part of the sumo wrestler's life is covered by kata, down to how such a huge man can perform his duties as a husband.

Sumo began as an oracular ritual performed at Shinto shrines to ensure good harvests. Over the centuries, it gradually became

Popular sumo wrestlers Hakuho and Bakuto in a tournament in Tokyo, Japan, on April 7, 2012. There are six sumo tournaments a year, each lasting fifteen days.

a spectator sport, at first still associated with shrines. Eventually local lords and bosses began sponsoring their own champions. Some bouts between the champions of competing lords were fights to the death.

The attractions of sumo have closely been bound up in its conformity to ancient customs and ceremonies. The giant-sized loin cloths the wrestlers wear, their entry into the ring, the ceremonial toss of purifying salt, the repeated confrontations between wrestlers before they attack, the squatting of the winner at ring-side, and the final twirling of the bow at the day's end are all part of the kata of sumo.

Sumo has some seventy precisely cataloged ways of attacking an opponent and either forcing him to touch the ground inside the ring, with anything other than his feet, or ejecting him from the ring. Only a dozen or so of the moves are commonly used, though. All of these precise moves are totally familiar to fans, and are commented on endlessly by sumo sports-casters.

Sumo became a nationally organized profession during the Edo period. There are presently six tournaments a year, each lasting for fifteen days, meaning there are bouts for ninety days every year.

Exhibition bouts are held in addition to the regularly scheduled tournaments, and in between tournaments fans may visit the different sumo *beya* (bay-yah) or "stables" to watch their favorites in training.

During the spring, summer, fall, and winter tournaments ,loyal fans, many members of the older generation, show up at the sumo stadiums.

The Shikata of Poetry

Writing poetry has been a popular pastime in Japan for more than a thousand years. The institutionalized custom may have been imported from China between the fourth and seventh centuries, but prior to this period Japan had professional oral historians along with storytellers and entertainers who often expressed their commentary in the form of poetry.

The introduction of the Kanji writing system in Japan between the fourth and seventh centuries spurred the writing of Chinese-style poetry, but it did not popularize poetry-writing among the masses, however, because learning Kanji was already limited to upper-class males. Teachers were strictly prohibited from instructing even upper-class women on how to read and write the semi-sacred characters.

It was not until the eighth and ninth centuries when a simplified phonetic writing system based on Kanji was developed, one that women and others were allowed to learn how to write, ultimately resulting in a massive outpouring of literature. The new system provided an extraordinary impetus for the leisured court ladies of Kyoto to make the writing of poetry an important part of their lifestyle.

Japan's first anthologies of poetry, written by emperors, courtiers, ladies-in-waiting, priests, warriors, and ordinary people, date from this early period.

During the heyday of the Imperial reign in Kyoto (794–1192), formally judged poetry contests were regular affairs. Ladies and lords of the court regularly communicated in poetry. Poetry writing became an honored profession, with titles and financial rewards bestowed upon the masters of the art.

After the usurpation of imperial power in 1192 by Yoritomo Minamoto, the first of Japan's shogun warlords, the members of the Imperial family and their huge tree of lineal relatives became a completely leisured class. They subsequently devoted even more time to poetry-writing and other aesthetic pursuits, setting an example for the still-larger number of priests, as well as the class of professional samurai warriors that had developed following the appearance of the shogunate form of government.

The more professional and accomplished the samurai warriors, the more likely they were to take as much pride in their ability to write poetry as in their skill with the arms of their trade. Fatally wounded in battle, ranking warriors would use

the last moments of their lives to compose poems, sometimes expressing their sorrow at leaving life before reaching their goals, other times pillorying their enemies with sharp poetic barbs.

Eventually it became the custom for soldiers about to enter suicidal battles to write "death poems"—a custom followed by the young *kamikaze* (kah-me-kah-zay) pilots of World War II in the 1940s. Just as other areas of Japanese life became kata-ized during the nation's long feudal period, the styles and rules of poetry were equally formalized and thereafter contributed significantly to the psychology and behavior of the Japanese.

Poetry certainly plays a lesser role in Japanese society today but it remains a popular pastime and each year tens of thousands of people, including members of the Imperial family, participate in a national contest.

Behind the Masks of Kabuki and Noh

The Japanese tendency to kata-ize everything in their lives was epitomized by the *kabuki* (kah-buu-kee) and *noh* (no-o) drama forms—the ultimate forms of method acting. Kabuki is said to have originated in the late 1600s as bawdy dances performed by Shinto shrine maidens attached to the Izumo Shrine in Kyoto.

Men eventually replaced all women in kabuki performances after the female dancers became as popular for their sexual services as their entertainment, and attracted the displeasure of the authorities for engaging in unregulated prostitution.

Eventualy male actors began turning kabuki into a fine art that became more and more formalized and stylized as it was practiced. Over the decades, master kabuki stars gradually transformed the craft into the meticulously kata-ized system that many people see today.

General Akashi Gidayu preparing to commit *seppuku* after losing a battle for his master in 1582. He had just written his death poem, which is also visible in the upper right corner.

After the form and order of movements of kabuki had been established by a master, the style he had created became sanctified. Every movement, down to the blinking of the eyes, was minutely prescribed for all of his disciples. Virtually no personal interpretation was allowed. The challenge for each performer was to follow the kata in every way. Success was based not only on the artistic interpretation of the plot but also on how precisely the player recreated the set form.

Eventually the style created by the greatest master became the universal kabuki standard and was passed on by him to his chief disciple. This cycle was repeated in each generation. The overall effect was that the kata of kabuki became as important, if not more so, than the story being told.

Noh, Japan's other drama form, which began in the 14th century as part of religious festivals, was to become even more stylized and kata-bound than kabuki. It developed into a form so esoteric that only a limited number of dedicated aficionados are attracted to it. The essence of *noh* is for the actor to merge his whole personality into the wooden face mask he wears, to physically and spiritually put himself into the mask, allowing himself to become the character represented by the mask.

This total sublimation of character and personality into an unchanging wooden mask, and making an art out of it, with the mask becoming both the medium and the message, was precisely the goal of all kata—and was characteristic of Japanese culture in general.

Kabuki remains one of the most representative forms of traditional Japanese theater and one of the more impressive examples of the ultimate kata-ization of an art. Performances at Tokyo's famed Kabuki-Za theater, the National Theater, and other locations continue to attract large audiences.

Anyone who has difficulty understanding the meaning and point of kata in traditional Japanese culture has only to attend

Noh theater tradition as presented by Reijiro Tsumura, one of Japan's noh masters. Noh itself is an excellent example of the power of kata in producing illusions and giving reality to the unreal.

a contemporary presentation of kabuki or *noh*. More severe foreign critics of the arts say they are virtually devoid of content and are little more than a shell. More importantly, they say, is that Japanese who attend kabuki and *noh* plays are not aware that most of what they see and hear is nothing more than form without substance. "What they are watching is not only meaningless, attending kabuki has become a kata within itself," said one critic.

Of course, this criticism presumes that there is no merit at all in art forms that are kata-ized to this extreme. However, both kabuki and *noh* are excellent examples of the power of kata in producing illusions, and giving reality to the unreal—both of which are vital ingredients in Japanese culture.

The Beauty Cult

One of the secrets of Japan's commercial prowess is its cultural emphasis on aesthetics. Very early in their history, the Japanese developed an acute awareness of the beauty in nature and later developed arts and ceremonies to incorporate the same quality of beauty into their daily lives.

These arts and ceremonies were soon institutionalized into kata with their own aesthetic vocabulary, making it possible for even the least educated person to study and understand aesthetics and make use of the knowledge. Japan seems to be the only country in the world in which there was a concerted effort on almost every level of society to make the study and appreciation of beauty a basic part of the lifestyle of the entire population.

The roots of the special affinity of the Japanese for aesthetics may have derived from their own native Shintoism, essentially a worship of nature that incorporated recognition of nature itself as the ultimate source of beauty.

Japanese people coming to see Sakura blossoms in Nakameguro, Tokyo. According to native Shintoism, nature is the ultimate source of beauty.

Another part of the Japanese impulse to universalize aestheticism obviously had its origins in Buddhism, as is evidenced in the arts, crafts and lifestyles that developed in other Buddhist countries of Asia. But no other national group took it as far as the Japanese.

It would not be too much of an exaggeration to say that from A.D. 700 onward, aestheticism in Japan took on the appearance and tone of a state religion.

Mundane crafts were developed into fine arts. The deliberate pursuit of aesthetic enjoyment became a major theme in the lives of the more affluent. The practice of one or more aesthetic skills became the norm and was expected of virtually all Japanese, regardless of their economic status.

Japanese aesthetic pursuits were designed to pleasure all of the senses and the spirit. They included such formalized practices as poetry-writing, moon-viewing, flower-viewing, incense parties, sightseeing, listening to the songs of insects, flower-arranging, music, folk dancing, and the tea ceremony.

By the beginning of Japan's modern industrial era in the 1870s, the Japanese had been immersed in an aesthetically oriented culture for well over one thousand years. The exercise of a highly refined aesthetic sense was second nature to them and was reflected in all their endeavors, from the weaving of baskets to the production of wrapping paper and soup bowls.

Unfortunately it was to be nearly one hundred years before the Japanese of the modern era could take full advantage of their aesthetic skills insofar as their export industries were concerned. Most of the foreign traders who began flocking to Japan soon after the country was opened to the West in the 1850s were more interested in cheap labor and the ability of the Japanese to copy foreign products than they were in their aesthetic sense or skills in producing beautiful handicrafts.

Following the end of World War II in 1945, the number of foreign buyers pouring into Japan to order cheaply made Western style products became a flood. For the next decade, the quality of what the Japanese produced for export was almost totally controlled by foreign buyers with an aim to make as much profit as possible as quickly as possible.

As soon as Japanese makers could wrest control of their production from foreign importers, by opening their own import offices abroad and establishing their own sales networks, they began to upgrade the quality of their products in keeping with their own traditions. Within ten years, the Japanese were renowned worldwide for the superior quality of their exports.

It was to be another ten years before Western business people began to show an interest in why and how the Japanese were producing such high quality merchandise.

I believe Japan's aesthetic concepts of *shibui* (she-buu-ee), *wabi* (wah-bee), and *sabi* (sah-bee) should be incorporated into all cultures. *Sabi* refers to a kind of beauty that comes with the natural aging of all things; *wabi* refers to the emotional appreciation that reflects the essence, including the ephemeral quality, of life; and *shibui* denotes beauty that results when an object, natural or man-made, clearly reveals its essence through perfection of form, naturalness, simplicity, and subdued tone.

The Art of Bowing

The bow is one of the most conspicuous symbols of Japan's vertically oriented superior–inferior society, of Japanese etiquette, and of the importance of social kata in general. Its traditional importance went well beyond simple conformity and good manners.

It was a significant part of both the physical and psychological conditioning of the Japanese in their whole culture. Until the 1950s, virtually all Japanese got their first training in bowing while they were still infants, strapped to the backs of their mothers. Every time their mothers bowed, the babies bowed with them.

Bowing correctly for different occasions is far more complicated and meaningful than the casual visitor might suspect. As in everything Japanese, there is a kata for bowing, with only one

Bowing is one of the most conspicuous symbols of Japanese etiquette. There is a kata for bowing, with only one right way for each occasion. Factors that determine the right kind of bow include age and the purpose of the meeting.

right way for each occasion. One must know when to bow as well as what kind of bow is correct for a variety of situations. The wrong kind of bow can be a very serious infraction with dire consequences. In earlier times, it was a fatal error.

The right kind of bow is determined by such things as the relative ages of the participants, their personal and/or professional relationship, their past experience, their purpose in meeting, and so on.

Older citizens, particularly those who are worried about the erosion of the Japanese Way, are especially concerned that Japan's younger generations are not being taught how or why to bow by their parents. As a result, many Japanese companies, especially those in the retail and service industries, now include bowing in their training programs. Some in the past have gone so far as to use a special bowing device to help new employees get the proper angle down pat.

Part of the worry of Japanese traditionalists is recognition that those who are not fully indoctrinated in bowing at a very young age have already lost a vital aspect of their Japanese-ness and will not regain it with a few days or weeks of training in the kata of bowing. These conservatives understand that the bow is part of the behavioral conditioning that makes the Japanese *Japanese*, and helps hold the traditional culture together.

Despite the tendency of Japanese parents to spend less time training their children in the age-old custom of bowing, it remains a vital factor in the adult world of Japan, and many of Japan's major companies are determined to keep it that way.

In the 1980s, many companies set up kata-ized training programs specially designed to wipe out the modernized personalities of new young employees and remake them in the traditional mold.

The remolding and character-building training programs of these companies were very intense. Some of them were degrading to the point that the previously pampered young recruits were shocked. When first established, the schools required new employees to do such things as wash out toilet bowls and clean up after sick drunks.

The primary purpose of these programs and special schools was not to teach practical subjects, but to condition the recruits in the traditional social etiquette still rigidly followed in the business world, and to instill in them deep feelings of loyalty and devotion to the company. Such training, which was usually very expensive, also made it perfectly clear to the new employees that the company was equally devoted to them.

This generally arduous, mutually shared training created a special bond among the recruits and between them and the company managers who often participated in the programs as instructors. The close ties they formed become a significant factor in the personal relationships of each new crop of recruits over their thirty-five to forty-year working lives.

In addition to acting as mentors to their younger colleagues, Japanese managers also routinely arrange marriages for them and serve as key speakers at their weddings.[3]

Until the late 1990s, many Japanese company managers looked upon college graduates with liberal arts degrees as ignorant, unreliable, and virtually worthless until they were whipped into shape at the company boot camp. In some companies, this "dirty work" training lasted for several months, and only those who survived the course were accepted into the companies as regular staff members.

Except for new recruits schooled in technical skills, managers did not look for the most intelligent, most ambitious or the most energetic employee candidates. In fact, still today young people who fit these categories may not fit into the typical company system in Japan. Many managers look first for young people

---

[3] One of the foreign-Japanese equivalents of mutually endured trials of strength, stamina, dedication, and determination are long hours of drinking and carousing in bars and cabarets after working hours required to forge close bonds with Japanese business people.

Building and sustaining close relationships in this manner represent one of the most expensive aspects of business in Japan—not only in terms of the financial cost but in emotional and time investment as well. Another mutual ordeal is playing golf when you have to travel several hours each way to get to a course and it is raining or freezing cold during the entire outing.

who do not have strongly held opinions or ambitions and can be molded into what the managers regard as company soldiers— people who will adhere strictly to the military-like hierarchy of the Japanese company, obey rules without question, and devote their lives to working diligently and rising slowly in the ranks.[4]

Female employees have often been excluded from the male bastion of higher management in Japanese companies, and are generally not required to undergo "boot-camp" training. Their training traditionally ended with how to sit, how to stand before superiors, how to respond with the proper speech, how to bow, and how to serve tea. Not surprisingly, Japanese women bow more often than Japanese men.

However, the government and many businesses nowadays want to see a lot more equality at the workplace. Better jobs and conditions for women can be an effective way of dealing with Japan's shrinking workforce, they reason. "We estimate that by closing the gender employment gap, the potential boost to Japan's GDP could be nearly 13%," stated a Goldman Sachs report, "Womenomics 4.0," published in 2014.

The idea caught on among a number of important people, including Prime Minister Shinzo Abe. The government went on to set "gender diversity targets" for large public and private sector institutions. While female participation in Japan is among the highest in the world, their presence in leadership positions lags behind most other developed nations.

The Art of Ambiguity

Another kata-ized formula that the Japanese have traditionally polished to perfection is the "art of ambiguity," which was devel-

---

[4] Major Japanese companies generally depend upon professors with whom they have strong ties to select the graduating seniors with engineering and other technical degrees that they hire each year. In most instances these professors literally decide on their own which student is going to what company.

oped to avoid commitments, disagreements, and responsibility, and to maintain a facade of harmony. It is also used to keep outsiders, competitors, and enemies uncertain and at a disadvantage.

Japan's cultural imperative to maintain harmony and promote group consensus by the use of ambiguous language had a fundamental effect on the nature and use of the Japanese language itself. The demands of being non-confrontational not only influenced the way the language was used, they also contributed to the appearance of new words and word endings.

The Japanese can and do, in fact, communicate clearly, candidly, and even bluntly to members of their own families, close friends and subordinates. But they automatically go into an ambiguous mode when confronted by anyone else.

The reason for this, according to Jiro Kamishima, professor emeritus of St. Paul's University in Tokyo, and a noted cultural historian, is that the Japanese suffer from a phobia about being isolated in any manner, physical or otherwise (*Japan Foundation Newsletter*, Vol. 17, No. 3).

Professor Kamishima says that the Japanese use ambiguity as a security device to prevent themselves from being caught in a minority position. He says they dread isolation from the mainstream so much that they refrain from expressing themselves clearly or taking a stand until a majority position gradually emerges. They are evasive, Professor Kamishima adds, because they lack confidence in themselves, and feel that the *seken no me* (say-kane no may), or "eyes of the world," are on them at all times. "They are obsessed with the idea that they must converge (their thinking)," he says.

This is one of the factors responsible for the development of the famous *tatemae* (tah-tay-my) and *honne* (hoan-nay) concepts in Japanese behavior. *Tatemae* refers to a front or facade (public statements) that people put up to obscure their real meaning and intentions (*honne*).

It is also the reason why the Japanese are obsessed with seeking more and more information and endlessly asking for advice from experts and authority figures.

Because of this, Japanese tend to be followers rather than leaders, going whichever way the leaning of their group directs them—and herein lies one of the dangers inherent in Japan's kata-ized culture. Like sheep, the Japanese are subject to being misled, either by misinformation or by a wolf in sheep's clothing. They are also prone to stampede in one direction or another as the result of a single incident. Their proclivity for jumping into fads is a part of this character.

The most frightening manifestation of this herd-like behavior is in the actions of Japan's mass media, which routinely tailor their approach to the news to conform to preconceived notions of what is "Japanese," or what is best for Japan. Generally speaking, individual news media that find themselves out of step with the majority will quickly fall in line if they come under sustained criticism.

Ability in using language ambiguously while still getting your point across remains one of the most important social, business, and political skills in Japan. Much of the famed *haragei* (hah-rah gay-e), or "art of the stomach" that the Japanese use in

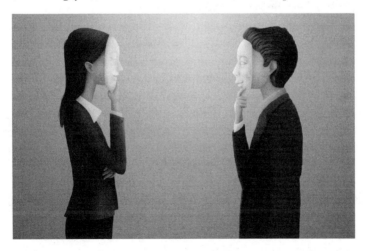

Tatemae and *honne* are Japanese words that describe the concepts in Japanese behavior. *Tatemae* refers to the behavior and opinions one displays in public, and *honne* refers to one's true feelings and desires.

their personal as well as business relationships, fits within the kata of ambiguity. *Haragei* is a highly honed emotional and intuitive ability that often cannot be expressed in words. It functions more or less like cultural telepathy, and is usually incomprehensible to those who are not similarly skilled.

"Cultural homogeneity makes it possible for the Japanese to communicate with each other without expressing their thoughts clearly or completely," notes American businessman-writer Davis Barrager. "Their comments and conversations are also regularly punctuated by blank spaces that leave the uninitiated listener hanging but convey volumes of unspoken thoughts to those who are on the Japanese wavelength," he adds.

This style of communication has been recognized and categorized for centuries. It involves the use of *ma* (mah), pregnant pauses, or "leaving space" that the listener is expected to fill in with his or her own interpretation of what the speaker means. Misunderstandings are a natural outcome when someone is unskilled at this kind of cultural decoding.

Barrager continues: "Many common Japanese words convey superficial meanings that mask reality. You must let communication with the Japanese run its course until something concrete emerges and then deal with it. Americans like myself, with our frontier traditions of dealing summarily with new situations, instinctively want to sift quickly through the chaff and go straight to the wheat. Usually that does not work in Japan, even when the Japanese want something as soon as possible. Generally you must let the chaff sift at its own pace."

When the Japanese are operating in their own cultural world, among themselves, they are often not aware of their use of ambiguity and time gaps. Most such behavior is automatic. Ambiguity is so natural and accepted that they generally don't conceptualize it, and often cannot comprehend why foreigners have such difficulty understanding them.

In formal situations, however, the Japanese are generally very much aware of the role of gaps in speech and ambiguity in all of their nuances, and are variously skilled in their usage. The deliberate use of this manner of communication has traditionally played a key role in virtually all of Japan's international relations, and remains an important factor today.

Of course, most Westerners who have contact with the Japanese are not skilled in the use of ambiguity or gaps in communication, do not accept it as normal and are confused and upset by it. This means that physically as well as emotionally, Japanese and non-Japanese are indeed often on different wavelengths.

There are other factors at play that make ambiguous behavior by the Japanese appear as irrational and often devious to the outsider when they have no intention of being or appearing illogical or deceitful. This again is part of the process of group-think and decision by consensus. During the investigation period of any project or program, no one in the group knows exactly where everyone is in the process. They cannot be precise in their comments or predict the outcome.

When judged by Western standards, the uncertainty and indecisiveness of the Japanese when they are in the midst of establishing a consensus adds substantially to their reputation for ambiguity and makes their behavior seem even more suspect.

Further, while Japanese find the use of ambiguity helpful in maintaining surface harmony and in keeping foreigners outside of their inner circle, the price they pay is high. It is emotionally demanding, and at least for those who have become partly de-Japan-ized, it is often frustrating as well.

The Importance of the Apology

Japan's feudal society was so hedged in by rigorously enforced rules of etiquette that it was virtually impossible for a person to get through any day without breaking at least one rule or rubbing someone the wrong way. The ritualized and sanctified manners also made the Japanese extremely sensitive to any deviation from this code of conduct, and ready to take offense at the vaguest hint of a slight or insult.

Just opening a conversation with someone other than a member of the household or a friend became a sensitive matter because it implied the possibility of creating some kind of obligation or invading the other person's privacy.

In a ying-yang kind of move to balance the demands of the etiquette system—as well as the often inhumanly harsh punishments handed out to the more serious offenders—the kata of the apology were institutionalized and made a significant part of daily life.

It became customary for people to apologize in advance—before a comment or action—just in case they might inadvertently upset someone or make a mistake. So common was the practice of the apology that one of the words used for "thank you" was also used to mean "excuse me," or "I'm sorry." This word—*sumimasen* (sue-me-mah-sen)—literally means "it never ends." In other words, "my imposition on you never ends."

More serious apologies were naturally formalized with their own kata, with different styles of apologies for different classes and groups of people.

Yakuza (yah-kuu-zah), or the professional gangsters of Japan, have traditionally apologized for serious transgressions against their bosses or other powerful figures by cutting off part of a finger—usually the first joint of the little finger on the left hand. If a second apology is required, the tip of the little finger on the right hand is cut off. It is still common in present-day Japan to see *yakuza*, with the ends of their little fingers missing, mingling with other guests in international hotels and nightspots.

Following the industrialization of Japan in the 1870s and 1880s, the apology became so important in the conduct of business that many companies employed professionals who specialized both in apologizing in person and writing letters of apology.

Still, today company managers who are especially skilled at apologizing are regularly assigned this task when the need arises. Besides having polished verbal skills, these expert apologizers must also be very good at performing the proper kind of bows and in selecting and presenting consolation gifts or money. The kata of the apology are therefore another critical factor in the complex conditioning that goes into the molding of a Japanese.

Despite their overuse, apologies carry considerable moral weight in Japan. The guilty individual who apologizes sincerely is often forgiven for relatively serious transgressions. By the same token, refusing to apologize or withholding an apology can be very serious. In legal matters, refusing to express regret invariably results in heavier punishment. In personal situations, it typically results in acts of revenge.

One of my foreign friends recounted a common experience, this one involving his mother. When out driving one day, she made a wrong turn and was stopped by the police. When it turned out that she had inadvertently let her license expire, the case became serious. Her husband, his employer, and the American Embassy became involved.

Things looked grim until a police officer came up with a compromise that let everyone save face. He told my friend's mother that all would be forgiven if she would write out an apology and promise never to drive in Japan again. The police officer then wisely added that it might come to pass that she would want to start driving again, but that no one could predict the future. He was giving her the opportunity to renew her license and carry on.

Big Brother and Groupism

Japan's social ethic during the feudal age was based on principles derived from Confucianism. All household and group members were collectively responsible for each other's actions. All could be, and frequently were, punished for the transgressions of one member.

This draconian system, which is designed to force absolute obedience to laws and kata-ized customs, contributed immeasurably to family consciousness and loyalty to the group, to passivity, and to robotic behavior. The crowding factor also made unified actions necessary, resulting in the Japanese tendency to move as groups in unison.

Each kata-ized group protected itself by threatening to ostracize any member who failed to follow prescribed behavior—a fate that was generally regarded as worse than death because other groups would normally not take an outsider in. The group thus defined and controlled the individual. In many ways any individual not a member of a recognized group simply did not exist.

Groupism is still a very significant facet of Japanese life. It prevails in every profession, in business and in politics. In most cases, getting acquainted and dealing with the Japanese professionally means getting acquainted and dealing with them not only as individuals but also as groups, with the group taking precedence over the individual. In business dealings in particular, it is vital to meet and nurture relationships with several individuals in the same company. Trying to work through just one person almost always fails.

The group, now as in the past, provides security and economic survival. There is relentless pressure for people to join groups and stay in them. One of the ways a group binds its members together is the sharing of personal, intimate information. Anyone who disregards this rule is suspect, and the more conspicuous violators are likely to be ostracized.

The Way of Suicide

To Westerners, perhaps the most bizarre and shocking facet of feudal Japan's kata culture was the practice of ritual suicide, called *seppuku* (sep-puu-kuu)—or *harakiri* (hah-rah-kee-ree) in colloquial terms.

The samurai class developed *harakiri* as a way for male members to dispatch themselves when an enemy caught them, when they ran afoul of their own lord or the shogunate and were ordered to kill themselves, or when they became involved in some kind of personal conflict for which there was no other acceptable alternative.

The terms *seppuku* and *harakiri* literally mean "cutting the stomach." This mode of suicide was chosen by the samurai because it required extraordinary will, courage, and strength to accomplish. A short sword was inserted into the stomach on the left side. Using both hands the sword was drawn to the right side of the stomach, then pulled upward, forming an angle or L-shaped cut.

Such a deep cut through the stomach was intensely painful, but it was usually several minutes to hours before the victims died. As time passed, it became common to provide for a quicker and less painful death by having an assistant stand to the side of the victim and sever his head with a sword immediately after the stomach cut was made.

In keeping with their highly kata-ized lifestyle, the samurai made *harakiri* into an equally formalized "art" that was as carefully and minutely programmed as a stage production. Every aspect of the suicide was detailed, from the white paper used to wrap around the part of the sword blade held by the hands, to the last poems the victims wrote before self-immolation.

Administrative castles, such as the soaring "white heron" hill castle of Himeji, had special inner "courts" for the ritual of suicide—appropriately labeled *Harakiri Maru* (Hah-rah-kee-ree Mah-ruu), or "Stomach-cutting Courts."

All official suicides required witnesses. The higher the individual's rank, the bigger the audience that attended the ritual. In 1868, Lord Redesdale, a British diplomat, and six other foreigners were invited to attend the suicide of a 32-year-old samurai from the province of Bizen who had ordered Japanese soldiers to fire on the foreign settlement in Hyogo (Kobe).

Lord Redesdale later recounted the experience in his book, *Tales of Old Japan*, the first description by a foreigner of this remarkable way of life and death. The foreign witnesses were both shocked and fascinated by the scene.

Harakiri was so entrenched during the long Tokugawa era (1603–1868) that repeated edicts by the various clan lords and shoguns prohibiting the practice were ignored. While uncommon today, the tradition of ritual suicide remains a discernible element in Japanese society, in attitude if not in practice.

The custom of *harakiri*, perhaps more than anything else, starkly reveals the depth and intensity of Japan's traditional codified culture and helps explain the reason why it was able to mold the Japanese into such a distinctive society.

The Kata-ized Mind

The introduction of industrialism into Japan from the 1860s and the disappearance of the samurai class after 1868 did not mean the end of the kata culture that had been so carefully and thoroughly nurtured for so many centuries. It was too much a part of the spirit of the Japanese to be so easily discarded.

The philosophy of the shikata system was an integral part of Japanese thinking, expressed not only in the use of their language but also in many of their deeply rooted habits and customs. It was the core of what made the Japanese *Japanese*. All of their attitudes and reactions, which foreigners tended to find either delightful or deplorable, emanated from this all-encompassing kata conditioning.

Japanese could not help but think in terms of shikata. It was this conditioning that was to make them formidable enemies in war and, from the 1960s to 1980s, even more formidable competitors in commerce.

Himeji Castle, sometimes known as the "White Heron Castle," had special inner "courts" for the ritual of suicide—*harakiri maru*.

3

Kata in Japan Today

Continuing the Kata Culture

At the end of Japan's feudal period in 1868, the custom of kata-izing all skills and behavior permeated virtually every aspect of Japanese life. The way to prepare and serve food was structured and codified. The way to hold chopsticks was rigidly prescribed. There was a set place to lay chopsticks when they were not in use. There was only one proper way to hold a teacup or sake cup and a prescribed way to drink.

Clothing was worn in a certain way that was taught as carefully as one teaches an art. There was a right way to fold and store clothing. There was a right way to dust and to scrub floors. There was a right way to hold and use a fan. There was a right way to walk. There was virtually no area of Japanese life that did not have a specific form and order. Any action or behavior that did not follow the prescribed form was not only uneducated and uncultured; it was un-Japanese and therefore anti-Japanese and by extension anti-Japan.

The downfall of Japan's last great feudal dynasty did not end the role of kata in education and training. In fact, the training system, which previously had centered on the samurai class and embodied many major kata, was quickly broadened to include the mass of common people as well.

During this period, universal education was made the law of the land. In addition to mastering all of the life skills in language and behavior that had been kata-ized for centuries, the lower classes were also now required to undergo the rigorous training necessary to master thousands of Kanji.

The country's newly organized Western-style military forces, made up of commoner soldiers and sailors, usually commanded by former samurai, were formidable examples of kata in action.

The armed forces were taught how to fight and how to die—but not how to surrender.[5]

Many of the other kata that were traditional in Japan for centuries were also carried over into modern times—some on a substantially lesser scale, but nevertheless to the extent that they make a measurable contribution to the skill levels and cultural coherence of the country today.

All of the massive efforts to transform the country from a cottage industry economy into a industrialized nation by importing Western ideas and systems during the 1870s and 1880s were filtered through the fabric of Japan's cultural kata, with the result that the country was modernized, but not Westernized. Some of the kata-based skills from the past that remain important today include performing the tea ceremony, arranging flowers, and engaging in sports like kendo and judo. There is a Japanized way to arrange furniture and office desks, for learning how to drive, for treating guests, for buying and presenting gifts, and so on.

Even the millions of dollars spent each year in the country's hostess clubs and bars by businessmen on expense accounts is a form of kata, says a female Japanese executive. "Most of the money is spent to impress customers and contacts, to obligate them and to build personal relationships that can be turned into business. It is not for fun or because they enjoy the company of the individuals involved. It is deliberate and carefully designed, with its own form and process," she said.

Japan's professional criminal class, the *yakuza*, have specific kata of their own that make them instantly recognizable to most Japanese. *Yakuza* kata cover their speech, the way they walk, their dress—even their hair style, with distinct variations based on where they live in Japan.

---

[5] Some seventy-five years later the end of World War II was probably delayed by several weeks because there was no kata for doing something that was virtually unthinkable. Some officers, quoted by Japanese author Hatsuho Naito in *The Thundergods* (the story of Japan's World War II kamikaze corps) who wanted to end the carnage bemoaned this lack, exclaiming "We don't know how to surrender!"

Typical *yakuza* wear pin-striped suits, black shirts with gaudy designs on them, lots of expensive jewelry including gold chains, pendants and lapel pins; have flat-top crew cuts or short Afro-style curls; walk with a swagger, talk roughly, are argumentative, and generally behave in an arrogant manner. Some 60 to 70 percent of *yakuza* have colorful tattoos that cover large areas of their bodies.

The Role of Martial Arts

Martial arts have had an extraordinary influence on the creation and maintenance of Japan's kata culture because of the development and long ascendancy of the professional samurai warrior class. Today, several of these arts, particularly judo and kendo, remain an important part of the mental and physical conditioning of a significant segment of the male population. Japan's modern sport of judo was derived from the ancient martial art known as *jujutsu* (juu-jute-sue).

Following the downfall of the Tokugawa shogunate government in 1868 and the subsequent dissolution of the samurai warrior class, many of the schools teaching fighting arts to the samurai were closed. Within a short time, however, martial arts schools open to the general public began to appear.

A Tokyo University student named Jigoro Kano got the idea of developing a form of *jujutsu* that anyone could practice as a character builder. In 1882, he opened the now famous Kodo Kan School of Judo and began promoting the new sport.

Kano changed the purpose of the art from disabling or killing an opponent to developing mental and physical control of the body and imbuing students with strong bodies, strong wills, high moral values and adherence to traditional samurai-style etiquette.

Kano's new version of a deadly fighting art grew steadily. Eventually it was introduced in regular schools as part of the curriculum, and also into the training at Japan's police academies. Now, as judo, it is a major worldwide sport.

Martial arts such as judo and kendo have been and continue to be an important aspect in the physcial and mental conditioning of Japan's male population.

While only a small percentage of all Japanese take up judo in school or as part of their profession—as in the case of police and the military—its influence is felt on a much broader basis because those who seriously practice the skill often develop the kind of character that contributes to their success in later life. The profiles of Japanese businessmen particularly show a higher than average percentage who practiced judo in their youth.

It is interesting to note that several hundred thousand Westerners have undergone intensive conditioning in Japanese kata since the 1960s, some of them without realizing the cultural significance, and the number continues to grow each year. These partially kata-ized Westerners are students of Japan's famed *karate-do* (kah-rah-tay-doh)—and most of them are good examples of the positive aspects of the kata system.

Karate-do, or "way of the empty hand," refers to a method of fighting based on using the hands and feet instead of weaponry. The earliest forms of "empty hand" fighting were created in China by Buddhist priests for self protection during the Tang Dynasty (A.D. 618–907).

Priests (and other common people) in China were prevented by Imperial law from owning and using any kind of weapon. Yet they were subjected to frequent attacks by brigands, the soldiers of warring lords, and various kinds of ruffians. Strong-minded priests developed the art of karate (as well as what is known in the West as kung fu) to protect themselves. Over the centuries the techniques of karate were expanded and polished into a highly sophisticated and deadly martial art.

In the 14th century, traveling Buddhist priests introduced karate to the island kingdom of Okinawa, now a prefecture of Japan, located about seven hundred kilometers south of the main islands of Japan. Karate thrived among the Okinawans but it was not until 1922 that it was finally introduced into mainland Japan.

As they do with all imports, the Japanese modified and Japanized karate, incorporating techniques and training methods from *aikido* (aye-kee doe) and *jujutsu*, both of which date back to the 11th century and the rise of the samurai military class.

Karate is a perfect example of Japanese kata in action in an ideal situation based on total control of the mind and body.

Also, as is typical in Japan, several schools of karate were soon formed by masters who favored slightly different techniques. The art spread rapidly among the discipline-minded Japanese, and from the 1950s began to attract the attention of many Westerners. *Karate-do* gyms can now be found all over the world, and the sport represents one of Japan's most successful exports.

In its modernized form, karate is divided into three distinct categories: (1) a set of defensive and offensive *kumite* (kuu-me-tay), or moves that are carefully detailed; (2) "free" moves, for offense as well as defense, in which practitioners may innovate; and (3) kata or "form" practice. Both of the *kumite* categories require an opponent, while kata is practiced alone.

The third category, kata, is the foundation of all karate training. Besides teaching the established basic moves, these kata are designed to condition the mind and the body of the student in an overall way of life. They incorporate control of the emotions, self-confidence, a strong spirit, respect for others, a sophisticated etiquette, plus a highly disciplined control of the body as it is put through a series of finitely structured moves performed at high speed.

Kata students cannot advance in rank without achieving considerable skill in the philosophy and discipline of the art. Normally, schools will not teach the deadlier facets of karate to anyone who does not understand and accept the philosophy and discipline that goes with it.

Karate is thus a perfect example of Japanese kata in action in an ideal situation based on total control of the mind and body, absolute adherence to minutely prescribed behavior, the mastery of techniques designed to mount a perfect defense or demolish an opponent, and a moral philosophy that integrates peace and power.

Survival Linked with Kata

Continuation of Japan's kata culture was guaranteed when the traits resulting from the kata were directly linked to the industrialized economy, which the new Meiji government sponsored from 1868 on. First, the level of schooling was made the primary qualification for employment, with the best jobs reserved exclusively for those who were better educated. Second, individuals who did not conform to the traditional way in both attitudes and behavior were rejected by the higher levels of the system.

Organizations of all types simply weeded out candidates who did not fit the national mold. Japan's tightly knit group orientation did not encourage individual entrepreneurship that might lead to conspicuous success by either the uneducated or social mavericks outside of the system. The relationship between kata-ized education and success in life became the overriding factor in the new Japanese society.

Official freedom to upgrade their social class through academic and economic success, virtually for the first time in the history of the country, gave the Japanese an extraordinary will to succeed despite the personal constraints.

Elementary and high school education in Japan was naturally structured with very specific kata that ranged from identical uniforms and bowing to strict routines for classroom performance.

The system was designed to mold each student into a homogenized product of the culture. The only screen for public college admissions was a standardized test. No consideration was given to school grades, extracurricular activities or anything else.

The overall result of all Japanese being subjected to a strict molding process during childhood and their teen years developed a common set of "Japanese" characteristics that were thereafter to play a seminal role in the country's future, more so than in the past because this time the system was applied to everyone, not just the privileged classes.

These characteristics included:

1. A highly developed sense of balance, form, order, and style.
2. An intuitive feel (and need) for precision, accuracy and correctness.
3. Extraordinary manual dexterity and the ability to work especially well on small, sophisticated things.

4. A predisposition to apply themselves with single-minded dedication to the task at hand.
5. An overwhelming desire to excel in anything they did; to be as good as or better than anyone else—although if they were better than members of their own group, they had to downplay their talent behind a mask of humility in order to maintain internal harmony.

Exhibiting pride in one's ability or accomplishments has always been taboo in Japan, and it is common to see noted people humble themselves before their colleagues and the public. There were no restraints on competing with other Japanese groups or foreigners, however, with the result that groups within companies as well as companies compete fiercely against each other. "No holds are barred. It is dog-eat-dog as long as a facade of harmony is maintained," said a resident foreign businessman.

In fact, within the context of their group, the typical Japanese citizen is virtually obsessed with being better and doing things better than outsiders, and is constantly making comparisons. A slew of books written by foreigners trumpeting Japan's successes appeared in the 1980s, and they proved popular with Japanese readers. Despite the plethora of bad news in the last couple of decades, the news media constantly reinforces the theme that the Japanese are a superior people.

In addition to the Japanese compulsion to excel as groups, it also became characteristic for each individual within a group to give his all for the group. The tendency was for each person to accept total responsibility for the goals of the group and do his utmost to achieve them. This results in an extraordinary amount of energy and synergy being applied to any project.

Despite the closed-in nature of the conditioning undergone by Japanese—or perhaps because of it—they have an eclectic mentality. As a rule, they are fascinated by foreign things and ideas, and have an innate compulsion to analyze and digest everything that comes their way. This compulsion covers everything from clothing and food to technology, and contributed greatly to the economic and social strides they have made since 1868.

Among other things, Japanese will sample any food, any fad, and if they like it they add it to their repertoire without any strain on their cultural character.

The Compulsion for Quality

Over the centuries, all Japanese were programmed with the idea that every service they performed or product they made had to precisely follow kata that led to nothing but perfection. No allowances were made for anything less. Time and cost were not primary considerations. Some of the more famous artists and designers of the day would not accept any project that had money or time constraints. This attitude remains characteristic of the Japanese today.

While virtually all Japanese workers are thus bound by the *bun* and *kata* of their occupations—as well as their identity as Japanese—to do whatever is necessary to make outstanding products, many Western workers have been conditioned to work efficiently to meet prescribed objectives.

As mentioned earlier, the quality of virtually everything the Japanese made for export from 1870 to 1960 was strictly controlled by foreign importers who brought the samples to be copied, noted the materials to be used, and set the prices. Japanese looked upon these products with contempt, regarding them as suitable for foreigners with no taste or quality standards.

Present-day Japanese are noted for their concern—some might say obsession—with quality, which is still another example of an important factor inherited from their kata-based culture. Their long history of kata-ized arts, crafts, and general lifestyle conditioned them to automatically expect the highest possible level of quality in any service or product.

In keeping with their cultural conditioning, the Japanese

began institutionalizing the concept of quality in modern- or Western-style products during the 1950s, and within a decade the whole process had been as kata-ized and sanctified as the crafting of traditional ceramics, lacquer ware, and pottery.

One of the aspects of the quality obsession of the Japanese is that it covers the whole product, including areas that are not ordinarily seen—the bottom, inside, and so on. Many of the foreign products that have failed in the Japanese market were not fully finished or detailed or were seen to have been built with poor quality.

Japanese-style Sincerity

Early visitors to Japan were singularly struck by the degree of sincerity, faithfulness, and fidelity of the typical Japanese—to family, friends and employers. The average employee would not cheat his employer or stint on his efforts despite lack of supervision or control. For the most part, dedication to duty and responsibility transcended personal considerations.

Present-day Japanese commentators point out that in many other societies, it is taken for granted that human nature is evil, and if not controlled will automatically resort to evil deeds—a belief that is usually self-fulfilling. In contrast, they say, traditionally oriented Japanese are intrinsically good and if left unsupervised will continue to work diligently, voluntarily trying to improve the quality of their work as well as their productivity.

Changing mores in Japan has frayed this traditional Japanese trait of self-motivated performance, but enough of it remains to be very conspicuous.

The sincerity and diligence of the Japanese is not a casual or amorphous thing. It is a structured, learned behavior that they take notice of and pride in. They habitually make comparisons

The crafting of traditional ceramics—black sake cups. The dedication in crafting only a single cup is an example of the Japanese obsession with quality.

between Japanese and foreigners, noting that Japanese are more diligent and more sincere than foreigners—while tending to ignore any evidence to the contrary.

A typical example of this behavior: At six in the morning, in a New York hotel coffee shop where I had just finished an early breakfast, I met the sales manager of a major Japanese company whom I knew from Tokyo. I made the casual comment, "You're up early this morning!"—a common greeting.

The man very seriously replied, *Kinbenna Nihonjin desu kara!* "Because I am a diligent Japanese!" His tone of voice and manner implied very emphatically that other people did not get up early because they were not diligent and did not measure up to Japanese standards. He simply did not recognize that many other non-Japanese, myself included, were also up and busy.

It seems to me that sincerity has several distinct meanings to the Japanese. A basic meaning is to never deceive one's self or others; to have harmony within one's inner self and with all interaction with others; and to precisely follow proper etiquette with the appropriate demeanor. Another meaning is to be constantly ready to give up everything in order to behave in a totally spontaneous way in response to one's innermost feelings. Such spontaneous behavior, when it occurs, can be either glorious or shocking, depending on its content.

As in all things Japanese, there is a specific, recognizable kata to Japanese sincerity. The fundamental ethic of Japanese sincerity is that people adhere faithfully to all expected behavior; that no action that would result in others losing face be taken; that decisions and actions reflect the will and needs of the group; and that harmony prevail.

Other key ingredients in Japanese sincerity include honesty, "wholeheartedness," "warmth," and the special Japanese characteristic called *ganbari no seishin* (gahn-bah-ree no say-e-sheen), or "never give-up spirit."

Showing Japanese-style sincerity requires that one follow the kata of Japanese etiquette and spirit in all things—eating, sitting, meeting people, talking, working, and responding appropriately to all the passages of life, from births and weddings to deaths.

The power of the kata of sincerity is demonstrated daily in all areas of life in Japan, sometimes with tragic consequences. On the day of this writing, five girls in a junior high school in Fukuoka were arrested and charged with bullying a classmate into committing suicide. When the five fourteen-year-old girls were asked why they bullied their classmate into killing herself, they said it was because she had "failed to be sincere enough" when attending a funeral ceremony for the mother of one of the five girls.

Studies show that Japanese business managers believe that sincerity takes precedence over all other management values, while American and European managers consider fairness the most important value. The next most important management value in the Japanese context is "the spirit of challenge," meaning that the individual is dedicated to giving his all to overcoming any obstacle and surpassing all others in achievement.

Because Japanese sincerity is based on a situational etiquette instead of universal principles, however, there is another side to it—an opposite, with parallel kata for being insincere when it suits their purpose. These kata include not saying what they really think, pretending that things are fine when they really are not, and ignoring things and people for self-serving reasons. This factor alone brings a very subtle nuance to interpersonal relationships in Japan, and makes it especially difficult for foreigners to have confidence in their dealings with Japanese.

Building Trust

The *shinyo* (sheen-yoe), or "trust" factor, in Japanese society is an extension of the sincerity factor. Without sincerity, one cannot have *shinyo*, and without trust, one cannot build or maintain a long-lasting personal or business relationship. Trust, the Japanese say, is the end result of sincere behavior.

Japanese are extraordinarily sensitive about "losing face," but this sensitivity often takes a backseat to their concern for trust. As is frequently noted, you can lose face any number of times and survive, and face is relatively easy to regain—sometimes in a matter of minutes or hours with some new success or redeeming behavior. But loss of trust is extremely difficult to overcome and there are many occasions when it is simply impossible to regain. As the Japanese say, not being trusted is like having a thousand and one enemies.

There is no mystery about how to build *shinyo*. In broad terms, one does everything possible to avoid disrupting harmony, causing someone else to lose face or giving anyone reason for doubting your sincerity.

In specific terms, one builds trust by keeping all promises and commitments. In business terms, this means keeping delivery dates, responding to complaints promptly and positively, making prompt repairs, and carrying out after-sales services. It also includes minimizing price hikes, notifying your business partners in advance of any planned changes and seeking their understanding and cooperation, continuously striving to improve the quality of your products or services, and helping your business partners—clients or customers—if they get into trouble because of circumstances beyond their control.

People who consistently behave in this manner command the trust and respect of all and can often get cooperation and help from Japanese companies that clearly transcends ordinary business considerations.

The kata of *shinyo* is nothing more than always following the highest Japanese-style moral and etiquette standards prescribed by the Japanese Way.

Not surprisingly, it is very difficult for foreigners to establish the kind and level of trust with the Japanese that they expect among themselves. Some life-long foreign residents of Japan say it is impossible. Even so, certain 21st-century business realities have loosened this attitude. Multinationals and other foreign companies, such as Starbucks or Amazon, have been making some impressive inroads in Japan after cultivating deep and extensive ties with Japanese suppliers or partners, who themselves are eager to become players in overseas markets.

A new crop of foreign business people based in Japan has found success by keeping a distinct distance from Japan Inc. Their small and medium-sized businesses operate on the fringes, serving Japan Inc., while not being an integrated part of it.

An American IT entrepreneur says his Japanese clients like to deal with his company, staffed mostly by foreigners, because it wasn't Japanese. "They want a piece of American IT," he explained.

Another American entrepreneur, who based his corporate training and development firm in Tokyo, advises against hiring old-school Japanese consultants.

"We had one who spent his time in the office thinking up all the reasons why our business would fail," he laughs.

Winning by the Numbers

Japanese are culturally conditioned to win and typically continue trying to win even though they know they are going to lose. They feel compelled to persevere because of the obligation they owe to their position and role in society, says Japanese writer Takashi Iwasaki.

This obligation is especially strong when the individual concerned is high-ranking—in the military, in business or in government—but it pertains to a degree to all Japanese regardless of their status. Ultimately, their identity as Japanese compels them to sacrifice themselves to fulfill the role they perceive as required to uphold the honor of the country.

The obligation to win or succeed in whatever endeavor concerned is, as always, group-oriented, but it is common for individuals of rank to assume responsibility personally when the matter is grave and on a large scale.

Westerners dealing with the Japanese invariably encounter this "must-win" tactic. In virtually all relationships it is predicated on the concept of continuing to talk and question (negotiate) in a very polite but tenacious manner until the other side compromises and a consensus is reached or the other side is worn down and gives up. This technique is particularly conspicuous in business as well as in political and diplomatic negotiations.

One veteran foreign negotiator observed that, generally speaking, the Japanese are exceptionally reserved and polite when they are in a weak position, but he added: "In my experience they are less polite and can be rapacious when they have the advantage."

Japanese typically employ a number of other deeply entrenched cultural characteristics in using their hang-in kata, particularly patience and pliancy—bending with the wind without losing their essence or form—and a strong, emotionally charged facade of polite humility, hospitality, goodwill and cooperativeness.

Westerners who are unfamiliar with this multi-leveled combination of cultural forms tend to be confused and frustrated when they are confronted with them as a concentrated force.

The Japanese approach to consensus building is a vital part of their negotiating technique and, planned or not, is often a significant part of their business tactics. This kata-ized approach requires that the matter at hand be broken down into its smallest possible facets or units, and that each of these bits be meticulously scrutinized from every angle to make sure everyone in the group totally understands the subject and has every piece of information that might be relevant.

This microscopic approach, which is reflective of training in Kanji, naturally takes time and demands a level of research and response that the typical Westerner regards as overkill, and often not worth the time, energy or cost.

To the Japanese, however, persevering and taking things a small slice at a time is the name of the game. Foreign businessmen, whether stationed in Japan or on a visit, who attempt to circumvent this deeply embedded pattern of behavior—by giving orders, holding a one-hour briefing session and, setting a deadline, etc.—are invariably frustrated when nothing happens or things go awry.

Generally speaking, there is no way for the foreign businessman to avoid this standard Japanese negotiating practice if he is the one seeking to deal with the Japanese. In that case, the best recourse is to learn how the system works and how to operate within it—which often means hiring a good Japanese negotiator who is conditioned to split infinite hairs and will do so on your behalf.

Traveling by the Numbers

Japan's awesomely efficient tourist industry is a very conspicuous example of their dedication to detail form and process. One of the most common sights in Tokyo, as well as other major cities and sightseeing destinations, is groups of Japanese students, farmers, and members of various associations moving about in orderly masses.

Such tours are scripted down to the last detail, including taking the groups to prearranged stores to do their mandatory shopping for the *mei-butsu* (may-e boot-sue), or "famous products" of the area. At restaurants everyone typically eats the same thing.

An American teacher who accompanied three thousand high school students on one of their annual outings said, "I don't think they (the teachers) allowed for one spontaneous second. Everything was organized."

Often, especially in the case of young students, the groups will be dressed exactly the same. They are especially conspicuous when it is raining and all of them are wearing yellow or orange raincoats and rain hats.

This sightseeing kata goes back nearly four hundred years and is a natural outgrowth of the Japanese way of doing things in a highly organized manner for the sake of efficiency as well as order. Systematic recreational travel in Japan began in the mid-1600s when religious groups called *ko* began organizing tours to distant temples and shrines as pilgrimages. Local neighborhood and shrine groups were formed for each major destination— Nikko Ko, Ise Ko, and so on.

These religious pilgrims traveled on foot, as did all other common people in Japan, and were thus on the road for weeks at a time when going to distant destinations. They moved in programmed formations that were as meticulously structured as military units on the march, following the dictates of cultural conditioning that had already been going on for centuries and was to continue down to contemporary times.

Even more conspicuous, and certainly far more important culturally, politically and economically, were the great "Processions of Lords" that were an extraordinary part of Japanese life for over two hundred years. This phenomenon began in the late 1630s when the ruling Tokugawa Shogun decreed that some 270 of the country's clan lords would maintain residences in Edo (present-day Tokyo), keep their wives and children there at all times as hostages, and themselves alternately spend every other year in Edo to attend the Shogun's Court.

This law—one designed to keep the clan lords under control and to prevent them from building up a strong economic base that might threaten the shogunate—specified how many warriors and retainers each lord could bring with him on his trips to the capital, how they would be dressed, their behavior, and the routes they were to take. The procession of the Maeda, the largest and richest of the clans, consisted of more than a thousand people.

For generation after generation, these great, colorful processions passed to and fro on Japan's roadways, demonstrating the power of the local lord and the ruling Tokugawa family, as well as carrying culture and homogenizing the nation.

Pilgrims hiking up the Daimon-saka. What began as religious groups organzing tours to distant temples and shrines eventually became the systematic recreational travel tours that Japan has become known for.

Remnants of such mass conditioning, still visible in such ordinary pursuits as recreational traveling, are yet another measure of the vital nature of the kata factor in everyday life in Japan—now also witnessed daily in countries around the world among millions of Japanese who annually travel abroad to shop, visit world-famous landmarks and honeymoon.

Reconfirming Japaneseness

My own favorite Japanese kata in action is a formalized banquet party called an *enkai* (en-kie), which is one of the most common and popular events in Japan. Participants in *enkai* parties are members of specific groups from companies, associations, agencies, schools, etc.

The parties are held at Japanese-style restaurants, inns, hotels, large banquet halls, and at hot spring spas.

Enkai banquets are perfect examples of Japan's kata-driven and homogenized group culture. Everything is carefully and meticulously carried out according to well-practiced custom—the seating, food, service, and entertainment follow a traditional format that goes back for centuries.

When the banquet party takes place at a hot springs inn (Japan has over two thousand hot spring spas) participants are often dressed in identical cotton *yukata* (yuu-kah-tah), which are robes provided by the inn. The entire program is orchestrated by a *kanji* (kahn-jee), or tour captain, and followed by the numbers. Everything that is done reinforces the group orientation, mutual dependence, and cooperative spirit of the group.

It is necessary to be emotionally, spiritually, and intellectually tuned to the Japanese Way to fully appreciate the meaning and importance of the *enkai*. *Enkai* are one of the primary "soul springs" of the Japanese, essential to their well-being in the

An open-air hot spring. Such areas can be a part of an *enkai* banquet party designed to reinforce group orientation and the cooperative spirit of the group.

deepest cultural sense. I have participated in hundreds of these cultural rituals and can attest to their spiritual and emotional impact, and to their effects in reaffirming the validity of the Japanese Way and their group-maintenance magic.

Virtually every Japanese adult who is well enough to get out of the house attends at least one *enkai* a year. Many, especially businessmen and professionals, typically attend one or more banquet parties each month. It is possible that the outsider who is not versed well enough in the Japanese language and customs to fully join in the *enkai's* ritual is forever barred from an important level of intimacy with Japan.

Enkai parties are a microcosm of Japanese culture in action, far more important to an understanding and appreciation of the Japanese Way than the aesthetic arts that Japan generally emphasizes to foreign visitors and tries to export.

Baseball the Wa Way

Not surprisingly, there is a kata for baseball as it is played in Japan. As the Japanese characteristically do with most things they import, they have Japanized the game to suit the national mind-set—much to the dismay of many American athletes who have played the game in Japan. In the process, they have made it into a topic that inspired two of the more entertaining and insightful books on Japan in recent decades: *The Chrysanthemum and the Bat* and *You Gotta Have Wa*, both by Robert Whiting.

How the Japanese play professional baseball is one of the best examples of their process and group orientation. On a Japanese baseball team, it is not how well you play, but how well you train and how you play that are important—a factor that totally mystifies and eventually frustrates most American athletes who hire out to Japanese baseball clubs.

On the one hand, American baseball players are hired by Japanese ball clubs for their hitting or pitching prowess. But the Americans quickly find themselves in a double bind if they do too well. If they show up their own teammates or the players on the opposing team, they may be deliberately handicapped to make it more difficult—or impossible—for them to perform as well.

There are a variety of the handicaps that have been applied to foreign baseball players to control their performance: taking them out of the line-up when they are having a hitting streak, enlarging the strike zone so pitches that would normally be balls become strikes (without explaining the new temporary rule to the batter), and replacing a pitcher striking out too many players.

The very "Japanese" point that most foreign baseball players cannot appreciate is that they are expected to produce on cue when there is no danger of anyone losing face. If they fail to produce when expected or do more than is expected, they are in trouble.

Another aspect of Japanese *besuboru* (bay-sue-boe-rue) is the extraordinary emphasis on the physical and mental training required by the managers and coaches. It goes so far beyond what American players consider necessary or desirable that they regard it as irrational.

Team Japan players posing for pictures following their 10–6 victory over Cuba to win the 2006 World Baseball Classic.

What is often even more disturbing to American players on Japanese baseball teams is the degree of togetherness and team harmony that is required. The whole team is expected to behave as a single-cell unit. The individualism and idiosyncrasies for which American players are famous are strictly taboo.

Another point that imported American baseball players are generally unaware of is that in Japan baseball is less of a game that is played for fun and more of a medium for developing and demonstrating spirit and harmony. In Japan, spirit, dedication, and discipline have much higher priorities than recreation and creativity.

No matter how skilled or how high the repute (or the salary) of the newly arrived American player, the first thing the Japanese managers and coaches may attempt to do is remold that player in their image. Their conditioning in the kata of baseball is so strong that their instructions to the new foreign batting ace may include how he is supposed to hold his bat.

This same obsession with form and process is repeated endlessly in every area of private and public life in Japan. It often works beautifully where automation and assembly lines are concerned, but when human interaction is involved it often requires an extraordinary emotional investment, slows things down and complicates matters.

Copying as a Cultural Attribute

From about 1870 until 1970, the Japanese were often roundly criticized as copiers instead of innovators. They were, in fact, geniuses at copying. But rather than this being a fault, their skill at imitating and adapting foreign customs and technology has proven to be one of their greatest strengths.

It was this same skill, among other factors, that gave Japan its technological prowess. Here again it was centuries of accumulated knowledge and experience, primarily gained through kata, that gave the Japanese an edge in becoming consummate copiers.

Kaizen is a unique word used to describe the ultimate goal of all of Japan's traditional kata, which is step-by-step improvement until ultimate mastery has been achieved.

It took the Japanese a while to develop the confidence to make improvements in the things they copied. Some of the Western products they duplicated for their own use prior to the downfall of the feudal shogunate in 1868 were faithful reproductions, including the design failings as well as the primitive workmanship.

As already mentioned, during most of the 20th century, when they were derisively described as copiers, almost everything they copied was done on order from foreign importers who, in most cases, were not interested in high-quality products.

Now, along with wholesale copying, the Japanese are among the world's most successful inventors and innovators because of their kata-oriented cultural skills and the added factor that the ultimate goal of all their traditional kata is step-by-step improvement until total mastery is achieved—an attitude that remains very much in evidence today and is summed up in the key word *kaizen* (kie-zen), which means "continuous improvement."

Dressing the Japanese Psyche

During several periods of Japan's feudal age, wearing apparel was generally prescribed by law, and what was not legally mandated was controlled by rigid custom. There was a prescribed dress for members of the royal court, the shogun and his court, the samurai class, and for merchants and other commoners. The date when people changed from summer to winter attire and vice-versa was officially announced—and was often at considerable variance with the weather.

The codifying of wearing apparel, based on class and occupation, was institutionalized to the point that wearing the wrong kind of apparel was a serious offense. Not only were the specific items of clothing prescribed for each group, the way clothing was put on, worn, and taken off, was kata-ized.

Centuries of conditioning in the right clothing and in the style of wearing it made the Japanese extremely sensitive to apparel, its style, color, and quality—sensitivities that remain big parts of the mentality and consciousness of present-day Japan. This attitude toward clothing carries over into all kinds of apparel, from business suits to sportswear. The kata for dressing combines with that of practicing or playing tennis or golf or whatever, making it mandatory that the person dress "right" for the game, meaning the "right" clothing and equipment.

Skiers and snowboarders who are on the slopes for the first time do not feel right unless they are dressed like professionals and sporting brand-name equipment. First-time tennis players want to look exactly like the world-famous stars who play before the cameras at Wimbledon.

Merchandisers of wearing apparel in general and sportswear in particular, along with sports equipment suppliers, have taken full advantage of these cultural factors in their marketing in Japan.

A fashion culture has developed around the Japanese schoolgirl look.

Cuteness and Infantilism

There is a shikata for feminine cuteness in Japan. This traditional kata consists of both girls and young women simulating child-like gestures and speech in a type of behavior that is highly prized by Japanese men as portraying innocence and virginal sexuality. Such contrived baby cuteness is a common practice among cabaret hostesses, is seen regularly in television commercials, and is carefully fostered in Japan's legions of teenage TV singers, known as "idol singers."

"Idol" refers to a phenomenon that began in Japan in the 1960s due to the overwhelming popularity of American music among young people. Because quality Western-style musicians and singers were still rare, the burgeoning new TV industry began creating entertainment stars virtually overnight to help attract viewers.

The primary focus of this effort was the systematic selection of rather cute girls in their early teens who were then put through a rigorous kata-ized process to teach them a specifically choreographed form to follow while singing and interacting with audiences. Standard choreography for each of the singers consisted of several dance-like steps and some simple hand movements, all of which were repeated endlessly during performances.

They looked and acted like cute little wound-up dolls. Many of them were particularly conspicuous to foreign viewers because they had one or more overlapping teeth, traditionally regarded as a beauty mark, perhaps because it was so common.

Few of the thirteen- and fourteen-year-old girls had really good voices and most were poor singers, but that was not the point. They were selected and packaged to represent role models, or "idols," for the millions of teenagers who were targeted as customers for their concerts and recordings.

The custom lives on today. One of the biggest idol phenomena is in the form of AKB48, which emerged in 2005. The concept here is clearly bigger is better: The "group" has over 100 female members—from their early teens to their twenties—who are divided up into multiple performing teams. The idea is that idol fans can always have the opportunity to see their constantly performing stars, including at meet-and-greet sessions.

The AKB48 members often dress in school uniforms—or variations thereof—while singing and dancing to their nearly entirely male audiences. As it was reported in 2015, the group had sold over 41 million records, making it Japan's most lucrative musical act.

The teams of girls sing in unison and dance in a highly synchronized fashion, underscoring a kata-based training and rehearsal routine.

Regardless of the act, packagers of idol singers know exactly what they are doing. The system is a huge success. There is a fresh crop of "new faces" each year, with most of the "older" girls going back to ordinary careers as high school students and, later after high school, company employees—their bloom of virginal freshness gone by the time they are seventeen.

In Japan, an infantile-cute kind of behavior has traditionally been sanctioned for men in their relations with women, particularly in the nighttime entertainment trades. In most instances when men go into the infantile mode, women automatically adopt a mothering role, whether the expected response is tender, loving care, or sex.

This cultural role-playing of infantile innocence by young Japanese women and Japanese men of any age is very conspicuous to Westerners who tend to see it in a very negative sense. It is one of the reasons why Westerners have traditionally underestimated the sophistication, maturity, and ability of the Japanese.

The Shikata of Being Japanese

A sense of uniqueness continues to permeate the Japanese. They feel different not only because of their historical isolation and the protective barrier presented by their language, but also because enough of their kata-ized culture remains to set them apart in a variety of measurable ways.

Globalization has arrived on Japanese shores, forcing many Japanese, particularly those in urban areas, to adapt. Some respond enthusiastically, by taking up foreign languages, traveling to exotic overseas destinations and aspiring to work for multinational firms. Others just shrug, viewing the transition as inevitable and a necessary part of their business.

However, most of those who have managed to live happily alongside or even thrive amid the changes are not so blinded, to the point that they renounce the culture of Japan out of hand. Many say the Japanese system still retains many superior aspects.

Extended exposure to Western culture also generally "taints" the Japanese to such a degree that they have extreme difficulty reverting back to their original Japanese character. After such exposure, they are often extremely critical or cynical of Japanese working conditions. Their targets might be excessively long hours at the office, subservience to one's superiors and office etiquette that appears to lack any kind of practical purpose. Returning to the Japanese fold, after long stints abroad or working at multinationals, often proves impossible. In the more traditional business and professional fields, they are often shut out completely because the kata-ized Japanese Way demands virtually absolute exclusivity.

Even so, foreigners who see the growing number of Westernized Japanese as catalysts for reforming the economy to come in line with international norms may have a bit more waiting to do.

Interestingly, the Japanese, especially females, are far more susceptible to Westernization than foreigners are to Japanization. Two or three years of living abroad is often enough to Westernize a Japanese native to a considerable degree. Foreigners often live in Japan for twenty or thirty years without any noticeable Japanization of their character or personality.

There are no doubt a number of reasons for the Westerner's immunity to Japanization. The kata culture of Japan is too intricate, subtle, demanding, and groupistic to be appealing to most foreigners. The system is also so exclusive that generally outsiders are not accepted under any circumstances, and the few foreigners who do make a serious effort to become "Japanese" only end up being rebuffed.

Many Japanese companies that assign staff overseas go to extraordinary lengths to help them maintain their Japanese-ness while abroad. This includes a massive amount of communication, far beyond that necessary for strictly business purposes. Some make frequent trips home that are more to sustain personal relations with their colleagues than to conduct business.

Until the late 1980s, part of the kata of being Japanese was an almost universal belief in the idea that entry into the Japanese market by foreign companies should be tightly controlled and limited, irrespective of any benefits to the Japanese consumer or any obligations of reciprocity the Japanese might have for the right to sell their own products abroad.

Still, today when confronted with this type of attitude and behavior, many Japanese will typically claim that the Japanese do not need foreign products, that foreign products are not suitable for Japanese, that foreign companies disrupt the harmony of the Japanese marketplace, and so on.

In the past, opposition to foreign-made products entering the Japanese market traditionally took a variety of practiced forms. The government or company involved would generally not oppose a specific product directly. One typical ploy was to delay things by asking questions, by doing more "testing" or "studying"—while in the meantime the company was sometimes gearing up to produce an identical product to the concerned in Japan.

There are still cases where larger Japanese companies, as well as government agencies and ministries, also systematically bring pressure against Japanese distributors and suppliers to prevent them from cooperating with foreign firms.

Another ploy that allegedly has been common among large Japanese companies is to contract with foreign companies in similar or related lines of business to distribute their products in Japan, then severely limit the distribution to prevent the products from become serious competition.

Many Japanese today have overcome this anti-foreign product syndrome, but many continue to believe that these foreign products in general are not suitable for the Japanese market until they have been properly Japanized. This feeling goes beyond anything having to do with size, design or quality. It is an innate symptom that goes back to the exclusivity of their kata-ized culture and serves them well in their efforts to "protect" the Japanese marketplace.

Behind the Bamboo Curtain

There is no great mystery behind the symbols that conceal Japan from the outside world—or for that matter, prevent the Japanese from seeing the outside world as it actually is. Kurt Singer, an educator-economist who lived in Japan in the 1930s, is one of many who have noted that the Japanese are hard to understand not because they are complicated, but because they are so simple.

Of course, Singer and these other observers go on to qualify what they mean by simple. In this case they are referring to the fact that the Japanese accept as normal contradictions and chaos that other people consider irrational if not mad. They go on to say that the Japanese do not meet conflicts head on and fight them, they avoid them, by compromise or by ignoring them. They add that characteristically in Japan, it is more important to avoid conflicts than to eliminate evil.

Public behavior in Japan, which is usually all the foreign viewer can see or understand, is designed to maintain harmony and allow time for things to be worked out behind the scenes. Things that cannot be quickly or easily resolved by consensus are usually tolerated until they change or die of their own accord.

In the same way, the lack of form and disorder that the Japanese perceive in the thinking and behavior of Americans and other Westerners is seen as a cultural and personal failing. It is also one of the key reasons why the Japanese consider themselves inherently superior to foreigners.

Dealing with Foreigners

Japanese have historically been unable to accept non-Japanese into their society. This intolerance goes beyond both race and language. People of Korean or Chinese ancestry who are physically identical to the Japanese, and whose families have lived in Japan for generations, and are totally assimilated into the culture are not accepted as Japanese.

The non-Asian person living in Japan, whether a citizen or not, is naturally more alien than Asians of non-Japanese ancestry. The idea of Caucasians, Blacks, and other races becoming "Japanese" is unthinkable. The world was reminded of that in 2015, when Ariana Miyamoto was crowned Miss Universe Japan. Miyamoto is half-black. Her win provoked criticism among some Japanese who complained that she didn't look Japanese enough, and thus should not be representing their country. The Japan-born beauty queen spoke to the foreign media afterward, vowing to fight old-fashioned discriminatory attitudes in her homeland.

As a result of such cultural discrimination, the Japanese have developed specific ways of dealing with foreigners, depending on circumstances and the different foreigners involved. These ways consist of attitudes and kata for dealing with foreign diplomats and politicians, businessmen, tourists, students, and residents. Regardless of the circumstance or who is involved, the fundamental factor is that the relationship involves a non-Japanese.

In the scheme of things in the Japan's eye, a foreigner is non-Japanese first, an individual second, and possibly a business associate third. This subtle discrimination permeates Japanese thinking and behavior, some of it subconsciously and some of it deliberately contrived.

The Japanese claim they do not discriminate against anyone. Their position is that they treat other Japanese one way and everyone else another way, and that they do not recognize this dichotomy as discrimination. The Japanese do not see themselves as anti-foreigner in the usual sense of the term. To stretch

an analogy, they see themselves as apples and non-Japanese foreigners as oranges.

To them, keeping the two apart is just common sense. "To be regarded as and treated as a Japanese, you have to be born in Japan, of Japanese parents, and raised as a Japanese in the full cultural implications of the word," says Japanologist Ken Butler. It is necessary to add that candidates for full Japanesehood must also not be members of Japan's own Japanese minority caste *(burakumin)*, whose ancestors slaughtered animals and worked with hides—which were used for armor.

Few Caucasian residents of Japan complain very much about being excluded from Japanese society. Author Donald Richie, one of the most perceptive observers of the Japanese scene, summed up the situation succinctly in an interview published in *Japan As We Lived It: Can East and West Ever Meet*, by Bernard Krishner (Yohan Publications, Tokyo). Richie stated that if he were a Japanese, he wouldn't stay in Japan for ten minutes. "The weight of (the) society on a person who is Japanese is very heavy," he said.

The truth is, until around the mid-1990s, life in Japan was only tolerable for most Caucasian residents because they were excluded from the society and treated differently.

Japanese have traditionally had separate policies and rules for dealing with foreigners, all originally designed to prevent foreign penetration into Japan or to minimize it and keep it under control. These policies and rules naturally are aimed at protecting Japan's interests—political, social and economic—and have nothing to do with fairness or reciprocity. While generalizations about the Japanese kata for treating foreigners are open to individual interpretation, there are some instances when it is obvious and undeniable.

Probably the most conspicuous example, mentioned earlier, is the Japanese attitude toward foreign tourists and their tra-

A non-Japanese person working in a Japanese company, whether they're a citizen or not, is a larger target of discrimination than, say, people of Korean and Chinese ancestry.

ditional treatment of them. As short-term visitors who are in Japan to enjoy the beauty of the islands and indulge in some of the attractions of the culture, foreign travelers present neither a threat nor a challenge to the Japanese.

This so-called "guest culture" incorporates an elaborate body of kata for the care and feeding of guests that keeps them impressed and happy for the most part, but also has the effect of isolating them from the realities of Japan.

Tourists are, of course, looked upon as guests of the country. The Japanese are masters at providing a regal level of service to guests, believing that if the guests fail to enjoy themselves and to go home enormously impressed with Japan, all Japanese have lost face. Foreign visitors who are recipients of typical Japanese hospitality are often tremendously impressed and become great fans of the whole country.

Encounters with all other non-tourist categories of foreigners cause the Japanese varying degrees of consternation. In the first place, communication is almost always incomplete and often nil because of the language barrier. In the second place, cultural differences in values, motivations, and methods invariably result in further gaps in understanding. Traditional fears and prejudices often intensify these factors.

One manifestation of Japanese distrust of non-tourist foreigners is a lingering innate suspicion of all foreigners who have more than a casual interest in Japan. This feeling is a holdover from the long era when every foreigner in Japan was believed to be in the country for ulterior and eventually harmful motives. Japanese are generally unable to give a foreign resident, student, businessman, or official the benefit of the doubt. He or she must prove himself or herself as friendly and trustworthy on a regular basis, from the first meeting on.

Proof of friendship and trustworthiness expected from foreigners by many Japanese, particularly those who are traditionally oriented, entails a kind and degree of behavior that often smacks of flattery, if not toadyism. Interestingly, many foreigners are so eager to impress and please the Japanese, for one reason or another, that they go overboard in their praise and actions even when it isn't expected or necessary. This latter type of behavior is likely to come across as insincere, reflecting badly on the foreigner and constituting yet another barrier to understanding and goodwill.

On the surface, it would seem that foreigners who speak good Japanese and have practiced behaving "in Japanese style" would be the least likely to create problems for the Japanese and have the most success in functioning effectively in Japan. This generally appears to be so in strictly social matters, but in business it is often not the case. The experience of one of my life-long friends is typical. After substantial "Asian" experience in Korea, he arrived in Tokyo in the early 1950s, determined not to fall into the familiar pattern of becoming either a hardcore Japanophile or Japanophobe.

His story: "I dedicated myself to disproving the theory that all *gaijin* (guy-jeen)—foreigners—in Japan had to either love the country or hate it. I set out to relate to Japan on the basis of total objectivity, and to do that by becoming totally fluent in the language, structuring my business and social life within the pure Japanese context and studying firsthand every aspect of the Japanese way of doing things."

"I pursued my program of total immersion for three decades. Japanism was my thing. No Kanji escaped my ever-ready notebook. The kata for any occasion, including hospital visits and funerals, became a knee-jerk reaction. I could lead business meetings in the Japanese language. I was as comfortable on the reed-mat floor of a Yanagibashi geisha inn as I was at Keen's Chop House in New York. I believed I was the optimum 'good' *gaijin*."

"I was certain that I had disproved the conventional wisdom of the old Japan hands which said that no foreigner, including third-generation 'born-again' Koreans—was ever accepted in Japan. I was frequently interviewed by the media about my experiences in Japan, and asked to write and speak about the country by prestigious organizations."

"I felt that I had reached the point that I could be both American and Japanese. I believed that I had crossed the 'gaijin line'; that I was accepted in both societies on an equal basis. Given this mind-set, I established a joint venture with a major Japanese company with whom I had already been doing business for several years as a supplier. The idea was to maximize the potential of the patented technology my company had acquired. My firm owned 45 percent of the joint venture; the much larger Japanese company owned the remaining 55 percent."

"I became the director of international operations in the new joint venture, and my long-time friend and drinking buddy from the Japanese side became the managing director."

"Much to my shock, I was immediately relegated to observer status. I was never asked to attend any management meetings. I tried everything I had learned about the Japanese way of doing business—the *ringi* (formal proposal documents), *nemawashi* (informal lobbying), and *nomi-nication* (drinking together in bars)—the gamut of culturally sanctioned practices. I brought in new ideas and new products. Everybody was polite and accommodating, but I was otherwise totally ignored."

"The new joint venture became extremely profitable, so in that sense I could not fault the Japanese side. But I was angered and frustrated that after more than thirty years of business experience in Japan, I was not accepted as a team member in a company in which I was a near equal owner. The awful truth came slowly and painfully."

"The old Japan hands had been right all along. Everything was fine as long as I was content to stay on the outside and be treated as a guest. With this realization came an understanding of the *gaijin* proclivity for becoming Japanophobes or Japanophiles.

"The Japanophiles—those who have not become deeply enough involved in the culture to learn that they can never be accepted—may be the lucky ones. The Japanese have kata for dealing with foreigners on the fringes of their society, but none for accepting them within their inner circle."

This old friend divided the Japanese kata for dealing with foreigners into three distinct categories: *gaijin no toriatsukae kata* (guy-jeen no toe-ree-aht-sue-kie kah-tah)—how to handle, treat, and deal with foreigners in business situations; *gaijin no atsukae kata* (guy-jeen no aht-sue-kie kah-tah)—how to handle foreigners in day-to-day arm's length relationships; and *gaijin no tsukiau kata* (guy-jeen no t'sue-kee-ough kah-tah)—how to relate socially to foreigners at parties and public functions.

He added: "Anyone considering any sort of commitment to Japan should be aware of these fundamental kata and the closed nature of the society, and expect to be treated accordingly."

Foreign women in management positions in Japan often present a special problem for Japanese businessmen, who generally have no experience in treating women as equals, much less as superiors. It is particularly difficult for such men to deal directly with foreign female managers because virtually none of the hallowed ways men in Japan communicate and commune with each other—using rough language, visiting cabarets and geisha inns, playing golf as an extension of business relationships—are considered appropriate for women.

The younger the foreign businesswoman in Japan, the more likely she is to upset the kata-ized equilibrium of older male Japanese counterparts. A young Canadian businesswoman, one who speaks very good Japanese and is a department manager in a major American corporation in Tokyo, said she found that un-Westernized Japanese businessmen had no idea how to treat her.

She said that when she took a younger, junior Japanese employee with her to meetings these businessmen would direct all of their conversation to the Japanese person, ignoring the fact that the junior employee referred all questions and decisions to her in Japanese and she responded in that language.

This same young foreign woman, who had majored in Asian studies and the Japanese language and spent time in Japan on a scholarship prior to going to work in Tokyo, recalled her earlier attempts to integrate into Japanese society. "When I came to Japan as a student I lived with a Japanese family, spoke only Japanese, went by a Japanese name, and learned all of the etiquette and special expressions that are a part of daily life. But at the end of a year, I was still as much of an outsider as I had been on my first day. 'My God!' I said, 'it isn't happening!'"

Because ordinary Japanese typically have trouble accepting bilingual, bicultural foreigners whom they have come to know and like, they often go to extremes in trying to explain the situation. Sometimes their attempts to rationalize how a foreigner could come to know and use their culture are bizarre.

One of the more common rationalizations is that the foreigner is actually "Japanese," despite his appearance. But if this self-induced illusion is shattered, they are disturbed. It is also characteristic of the Japanese to refer to foreigners who know Japan well as *wakarisugiru* (wah-kah-ree-suu-ghee-rue), or as "knowing too much." The term is frequently used in a friendly or joking manner, but it nevertheless expresses the built-in fear the Japanese have of being exposed or becoming understandable to outsiders.

The Japanese requirement for continuously proving one's loyalty and commitment to Japan is not limited to foreigners. The Japanese themselves must constantly reaffirm their Japanese-ness in numerous ways—by following certain customs, eating certain foods, taking acceptable positions on issues, and so on. This reaffirmation is both private and public and is part of the Japanese process of maintaining their identity and mental health.

One of the most controversial issues facing Japan today is the way foreign residents are treated, especially those who have migrated to the country illegally to find jobs. I was among the first few foreigners to be hired full-time—but not as regular employees with benefits—by Japanese companies following the end of World War II. By the mid-1950s, several hundred English-speaking foreigners had been engaged by Japanese firms on a temporary basis, primarily as English teachers, writers, and editors.

This pattern was to continue for the next several decades, by which time there was growing pressure both internally and externally for Japanese companies to at least make a token move toward liberalizing their employment practices. The growing globalization of business in Japan—on the manufacturing, retailing and exporting levels—made it increasingly obvious that many Japanese companies could clearly benefit from having some foreign employees.

The idea of Japan adopting a large-scale type of immigration policy, as found in Western countries, has been bandied about over the years.

Brazilians of Japanese descent were starting to become Japan's largest immigrant group from early in the 21st century. A loosened immigration rule allowed these Latin Americans to come as guest workers, with family members in tow, to labor in the automotive and electronics industries, engaged in arduous low-paid labor that few young Japanese were willing to do. Their communities tend to be in industrial areas in provincial parts of the country. An especially large community is in Aichi Prefecture, where factories supplying Toyota Motor are concentrated.

As the communities spread and started to lay down roots, it seemed Japan was finally coming to terms and ready to accept full-fledged immigration and the people such policies create.

But then came the global financial crisis of 2008. Japanese automotive and electronics exports plummeted, and the jobless rate approached 5 percent, low by most other countries' standards, but shockingly high for Japan.

Some Brazilians decided to leave. Others decided not to. They had settled here with their families, after all, and were willing to wait out the economic cycle.

Japanese government officials had a problem appreciating that state of affairs. They decided that lots of the jobless ones needed to go home without delay. They offered each immigrant worker $3,000, and $2,000 per dependent, for air tickets home. In the fine print of the application forms was one big condition: the recipients were barred from coming back to Japan until its economy improved.

Not surprisingly, the policy was blasted by immigration-advocacy and human-rights groups (although many regular Japanese citizens weren't particularly bothered by it). The incident cemented the idea that Japan—both its government and the people at large—really don't like the idea of sharing their communities and country with large numbers of newcomers and are willing to endure a possible drop in living standards to maintain the status quo.

The incident also highlighted the ineptitude of Japan's immigration officials. They had bizarrely assumed that the Latin Americans' "Japanese blood" would somehow make them automatically assimilate, despite being born and raised in a culture distinctively different from Japan's. There were in fact friction and flare-ups between members of the immigrant communities and their Japanese neighbors.

The business community, however, has been a leading advocate of stepped-up immigration, notably the Japan Federation of Employers Association, or "Keidanren." And no wonder; business owners in Japan are struggling with a shrinking domestic market in tandem with a smaller and smaller working-age population. Foreign workers who are fully integrated to Japan and its business practices should be able to fill at least some of the ranks of Japanese companies at operations both at home and abroad, many believe.

An area where these managers see a lot of potential is Southeast Asia. The economies there have been about as robust as Japan's has been sluggish. In addition, more and more students from the region have been enrolling in universities and colleges in Japan, and some employers view these young foreigners—who speak Japanese, are friendly toward Japan, and well acquainted with its culture—as rich pickings.

In 2016, Kyodo News reported on how one Tokyo-based recruitment agency, ASEAN Career, was catering to the needs of Japanese businesses "eager to hire people in the region." The agency had over 2,500 people from such countries as Thailand and Vietnam registered in its data bank, according to the article.

The site's operator, Node Inc., was sponsoring job fairs, where potential employers and employees could meet face to face.

One of the several reasons given by the Japanese for not routinely hiring foreigners who have skills they need is that since foreigners generally do not know and cannot follow the Japanese Way, they are unpredictable and would cause more problems than they would solve. Interestingly, this excuse is rapidly losing its justification, however, as more and more of the foreigners seeking white-collar work in Japan do speak Japanese and are familiar with the culture.

The close-knittedness and security provided by Japan's web of kata have made the Japanese exquisitely sensitive to anything unexpected. They cannot stand for things to be unpredictable, which is one of the reasons why those who are un-Westernized are so uncomfortable when dealing with foreigners.

Because they cannot predict what foreigners are going to say or do, such Japanese are under constant stress when in their presence. These factors are often further complicated when some older Japanese are concerned because they take special pride in their Japaneseness and work very hard at it, sometimes to the extent that their pride and prejudices outrun their common sense. Naturally enough, these people are the most difficult for Westerners to understand and deal with.

One life-long foreign resident of Japan said the Japanese habitually retreat into ceremonious formality when they face any unfamiliar situation, and that ceremony is also used as an escape from reality. "Kata have, in fact, traditionally been used to replace honest human relationships," he said.

The same observer added that the social etiquette the Japanese developed to support the shikata system doesn't fit in the modern world, but that without kata the Japanese are lost and do not know how to behave. "From a Western viewpoint the Japanese have been dehumanized by their dependence on kata," he added.

Kata in Politics

Not surprisingly, the form and order of Japanese politics follow traditional patterns of behavior, meaning that the system is based on groupings (factions) rather than true party lines or clear political principles; members of these individual groups are arranged in a hierarchical order; seniority and longevity generally take precedence over character and talent; and decisions are based on a consensus within the factions or among them when the cooperation of other factions is necessary.

The largest and strongest of the factions tend to monopolize the positions of privilege and power, but very little authority is invested in individuals or in offices. Government policy-making on both a national and prefectural level is more or less a group effort with several groups contending against each other, while the day-to-day administration of the prefectures and national affairs is left to bureaucrats.

This system obviously works well enough within the Japanese context of things that it—along with the whole culture—has survived for a long time. But it ranges from only partly effective to hopeless when trying to deal with international affairs because there is no central position of power and the foreign side is unable to deal with it effectively.

At the end of the 1980s, a series of scandals involving ranking politicians and businessmen resulted in a national outcry for a reformation of the Japanese political system. A series of political reforms went ahead in subsequent years, and seemed to have an impact. The scandals obviously didn't go away, but clearly died down in the aftermath.

Some of the formulas used by Japan's Ministry of Foreign Affairs in its relations with the American Embassy in Tokyo are indicative of how the culture is manipulated to benefit the Japanese. Virtually all of the Ministry of Foreign Affairs personnel directly involved with the U.S. speak good or passable English.

The Japanese make sure that the joint study programs sponsored by the embassy and Ministry of Foreign Affairs are conducted in English. Practically all of the informal conversations between Ministry of Foreign Affairs and Embassy personnel at the continuous round of parties are also in English.

This makes it possible for Japanese diplomats to say what the foreign side likes to hear, but to keep their comments completely divorced from the reality of the Japanese attitude and position when it serves their purpose. Part of the psychology is that whatever they say in English doesn't count.

The same psychology generally applies in all situations. Bilingual Japanese regularly say and write all kinds of things in English and other foreign languages that they wouldn't dare express in Japanese. By the same token they customarily express opinions in Japanese that are strictly for Japanese consumption, and tend to become very upset when such comments are published in other languages.

Interestingly, the Japanese generally do not see anything immoral or unprincipled in basing their comments and behavior on the language they are speaking. Many readily admit that such duplicity is necessary because the Japanese side would not understand or would get angry—or in other cases, because the foreign side would react in an undesirable way.

The factor at play in this situation is that the Japanese perceive their own reality as differing from foreign reality, that each is in its own dimension, and that mixing the two is either uncalled for or dangerous. They are able to consistently control most meetings with their foreign counterparts because the foreign side usually does not speak Japanese well enough to communicate fully in the language and either accepts what the Japanese say or remains frustrated.

One of the most obvious barriers used in to keep foreigners away from the inner workings of Japan's politics and economy is the notorious "press clubs," which traditionally barred foreign journalists from having equal access to news sources. Each of the key news sources in the country, from the prime minister's office to major corporations, has a press club made up of selected members of the Japanese press.

Until the 1990s, foreign journalists could not join the clubs, and until the 1980s could not attend press conferences arranged by the clubs or the news sources—unless they were separate meetings arranged especially for foreign reporters.

The Japanese rationale for barring foreign reporters from their press conferences was simple: They said the sessions were conducted in Japanese, but only a few if any of the foreign journalists could actually speak it. Foreign journalists would most likely misunderstand the statements and policies of the business and government spokespeople because their comments were made for a Japanese audience; and since foreigners did not understand the Japanese way of doing things, the journalists would be unable to accurately report on the proceedings and would create problems between Japan and the world at large, and so on.

It took nearly forty years of pressure—and fundamental changes in Japan's culture—before this extraordinary barrier was even partially breached.

The Layered Culture

In the Japanese scheme of things, as already mentioned, aesthetic values, harmony, and maintenance of the correct order of things can take precedence over what the West tends to regard as ethical and moral principles. This concept underpins many of the political and business policies followed by Japan today that Westerners view as irrational.

The built-in need for avoiding disruptions of any kind is also partly responsible for the Japanese habit of importing foreign ideas and things, categorizing them and keeping them separate from traditional Japan. This approach has allowed them to graft layers of foreign culture onto their own without losing their own distinctive ways.

Japan has never imported Western technology with the idea of changing its system to be more like that of the West. Its importation of Western know-how was first based on the concept of protecting Japan from inroads by foreign powers, and then, later, on continuing to enhance its competitive position on the international scene.

Despite Japan's copious borrowings from Korea and China in the past and the advanced Western nations of the present, once the Japanese have imported an idea, a custom, or a product, they transform it into something that is different, with a certain Japanese-ness that is always present. No sensitive person can spend more than a few days in Japan without realizing that Japanese culture has a style and a sense of its own that is a significant factor in the strength of the country.

Foreigners can live a lifetime in Japan, however, and not fully understand how the Japanese system works the way it does. Japanese culture, unlike much of Western culture, is not always open and visible, and does not travel well. At the same time, Japanese culture can be discarded in a short period of time, while Western culture is difficult to shed. Life within Japanese society is indeed like a silken web, often times incandescently beautiful to the outsider, but bonds of steel to those caught up in it.

Most of Japan's perceived internationalization or Westernization is a facade that touches the skin, but does not penetrate it. They may dress Western and eat Western, and occasionally behave Western, but for the most part they continue to think and act in a distinctively Japanese manner. They are very sensitive about these differences and comment on them constantly.

Still today most Japanese automatically express wonder when a foreigner demonstrates even the smallest "Japanese-like" skill, whether it is the Japanese language or the use of chopsticks. Their reaction is an instinctive, kata-ized response that eventually becomes very irritating to long-time foreign residents, especially to those who do speak the language well and have been using chopsticks routinely for several decades. Said one: "It makes me feel like a trick monkey."

This typical reaction of the Japanese is another reason why many foreigners, who don't really know them, have traditionally regarded the Japanese as intellectually inferior.

There are many daily examples of the extraordinary hold that traditional Japanese culture continues to have on the average person. One of the most telling is when they demonstrate an innate inability to fully accept even the slightest, invisible differences between a "true" Japanese and anyone who has been touched by some aspect of non-Japanese influence.

When Japan was forcibly opened to commerce with the West in the 1850s by the U.S., the Japanese very quickly made a clear distinction between what they wanted to import from the West and what they wanted to avoid. They saw themselves as far more cultured than Westerners and far superior in spirit, but seriously lacking in academic and technological knowledge.

They immediately began a massive program of bringing in foreign educators and technicians to help them industrialize their economic infrastructure—a stupendous feat that was accomplished in less than twenty years in large part because of their spirit and kata conditioning—and a feat that they were to repeat between 1945 and 1960, the period when they rebuilt their economy from the ashes of World War II, again with the massive use of foreign technology and know-how.

Becoming International

The Japanese are acutely aware they need to interact with the world if they are to remain a global player. They are even more aware of the cultural chasm that separates them from the West, in addition to China, India and elsewhere in Asia. Many are changing their way of thinking and doing things in order to work with foreign partners and customers.

In addition to this economic and political pressure to change, there has also been growing social pressure emanating from those who were born after 1960 and have not been fully Japanized. These combined factors resulted in a movement that was prominent in the 1980s and was generally referred to as *kokusai-ka* (koke-sie-kah) or "internationalization." This was a catch-all phrase covering any move away from traditional Japanese attitudes, behavior and styles. Over subsequent years, the concept became heard less frequently and discussions shifted toward globalization.

The internationalization movement was more style and form than substance. But among the young in particular, the desire was real enough and they used to spend enormous amounts of money and time engaging in "international" activities that ranged from studying English, traveling abroad and eating Western or "ethnic" style foods (Thai, Indian, etc.), or shopping in exclusive boutiques. Eventually, such activities became so widespread as to be taken for granted, and a label was no longer necessary to describe them.

4

Kata in Business

Learning the Roles and Rules

K NOWLEDGE of kata that apply in business and professional relationships in modern-day Japan—along with skill in using them and being able to predict their effects—is especially critical for Japanese as well as foreigners because it is in the business and professional worlds that the kata culture is the strongest. Key kata in these areas, more or less in the order in which they come into play, include the following:

Aisatsu no shikata (Aye-sat-sue no she-kah-tah).

This is the formal Japanese way of greeting or acknowledging other people. *Aisatsu* by itself is usually translated as greeting, but when used in its full form, it covers an abundance of important social etiquette, such as using third parties as go-betweens, bowing and exchanging name-cards, and using the right level of language at the right time.

The initial *aisatsu*, as well as subsequent behavior, is directly influenced by your own perceived status in the sense of social class and business or professional rank, age, and so on. These factors play a role concerning whom you qualify to meet, how you can/should behave toward them, and the treatment or response you can expect from them.

There are numerous occasions when businessmen and other professionals are expected to make formal *aisatsu* visits to suppliers, clients, and others with whom they have a relationship. These occasions include weddings, deaths, New Year's parties, a change of positions, when serious mistakes or accidents occur, and when transferring to a new location.

Sometimes the concept of aisatsu calls for the presentation of gift money, such as *otoshidama*, which is the custom of giving money to children on the first day of the New Year.

Presenting money to people doesn't just apply to children; money is also provided to the family of a deceased one. This custom is called *koden*.

Aisatsu can change with the circumstances. Some call for the presentation of gifts or condolence money; others include congratulations, formal expressions of appreciation, and so on. All require use of various levels of *keigo* (kay-e-go), or formal Japanese, the right kind of demeanor, the right degree of bowing.

Accomplishing *aisatsu* properly is an exercise in a broad spectrum of Japanese culture, including the kata-ized way the language is used, the appropriate tone of voice and facial expression, the positioning and moving of the body, and the underlying Confucian philosophy of respect for authority and seniority.

Skill in performing aisatsu does not come easily. It requires considerable knowledge and deliberate practice.

Aisatsu and its role in Japanese behavior should not be ignored or taken lightly by foreigners. It is a vital form of communication and as much of a skill as professional acting.

Denwa no kakekata (Dane-wah no kah-kay-kah-tah)

This is literally "how to use the telephone," which includes not only what you say, but how you say it. In business and other formal situations, Japanese are acutely sensitive to language usage because both the level of the language and the way it is used are directly related to the social and professional rank of the individuals involved, and to maintaining proper position and harmony.

Before one can determine which level of language and what tone of voice is appropriate for a given situation, it is necessary to know a lot about the other individual—their age, their company status, their educational level, social status, and so on. If you telephone someone you know, you naturally adopt the "right" *kakekata*. If you are calling someone with whom you do not already have a well-defined relationship, it is important that you use a relatively high level of language.

Been taught from childhood onward the significant etiquette of bowing, it is common for someone to bow even when they are talking to someone on the phone.

Generally, the Japanese will accept non-Japanese telephone etiquette from unknown foreign telephone callers if the callers are polite in a general sense, but they remain especially sensitive to disembodied contacts in which normal physical etiquette is not possible. It is still common for people who have been drilled in Japanese behavior from childhood to bow, sometimes repeatedly, when they are talking to someone on the phone.

Japanese traditionally didn't do business of any kind with anyone whom they had not met face-to-face and established a fairly close relationship. Email and mobile phones quickly changed that in many fields, particularly media and the IT industry.

Even so, proper formal introductions are usually required in most other areas of business. Making the initial contact by phone—to get an appointment to introduce yourself and begin the process of establishing the necessary relationship—is accepted, but requires considerable skill (especially when the caller is Japanese) in the use of polite forms of the language, in explaining where and how you got the other party's name and why you are calling in the first place.

Salesmen have to be especially skillful in using polite Japanese to avoid upsetting prospects and to get appointments with people they want to see. Listening to one of these polished professionals on the phone is a course in Japanese psychology.

Foreign businessmen doing their own telephoning in Japan are generally treated with some tolerance. How their calls are handled depends on whether or not they speak Japanese well enough to communicate or if they can get someone on the phone who speaks their language. The next factor is whether they have an introduction to a specific individual in the company. If so, they can usually get to that person or at least to a staff member who will take a message.

Foreign callers who do not speak Japanese take a chance that whoever answers the phone speaks enough of their language to communicate with them, or will quickly get someone who can on the phone.

Most Japanese companies heavily engaged in international business have personal assistants or receptionists who speak fairly good to good English, but more traditional Japanese companies do not.

If the foreign caller has an introduction that is "strong" enough, the individual concerned will probably see him regardless of what he wants. If the foreign (or Japanese) caller does not have an introduction to a specific person, he may be connected to someone in the General Affairs Department of the company, which handles a variety of miscellaneous activities. It is much wiser—and expected—that callers find out in advance who is in charge of their area of interest.

Denwa no ukekata (Dane-wah no uu-kay-kah-tah)

Not surprisingly, there is also a kata for answering phone calls, but how carefully the established form is followed varies with the standards and training of the individuals and companies concerned. Another factor is whether a mobile or landline phone is used. Because callers are not visibly present, this is one area where kata is often ignored by people who are not controlled by their employer or their own standards.

The higher the status/rank of the caller, the higher the form of polite Japanese that is expected from the person answering the phone. Until the status of the caller is established it is therefore important that a respectable level of etiquette be used.

One of the set phrases used when answering telephone calls, *Itsumo osewa ni natte imasu* (Eet-sue-moe oh-say-wah nee nottay ee-mahss), is designed to cover almost any situation It more or less means "I/we are always being looked after by you," and is more or less an apology in this context. It also has the connotation of "You're always helping me/us" (and we're grateful). This way, no matter who is calling, for whatever purpose, they are made to feel that the call is welcome and that there is some obligation to serve the caller.

Female staff members of larger corporations have to be especially careful about using the proper level of polite Japanese when they answer the phone. Their own male colleagues as well as male callers, particularly those of higher rank, typically judge them as well as the company by how they answer the phone.

Mobile phone calls typically follow a compressed version of the traditional or standard approaches done on landline phones. After a quick introduction, the caller should always ask the other party whether they are available to speak before launching into the conversation, and if they are not, ask for a convenient time to call back.

Although the proliferation of mobile phones has contributed to a more casual approach to business communications, the Japanese exercise considerable fidelity to callers and attention to protocol. Voicemails and calls that are not picked up because the person is in a meeting or simply driving are nearly always responded to at the earliest moment. Delaying such a response can be considered bad form, especially if an important client is involved.

A common observation made by foreign residents is the sight of Japanese people, usually dressed in business suits, bowing as they speak into their mobile phones, including times while they're speaking in crowded areas like train stations.

This is often a source of amusement, but ironically many of those foreign observers will eventually find themselves doing the exact same thing once they've learned to speak a decent level of Japanese and become more assimilated with Japanese business practices.

Email exchanges also require similar levels of fidelity and protocol as phone calls. If you make an inquiry, you can normally expect a prompt response, sometimes within seconds. And of course, you're expected to reciprocate this kind of courtesy and consideration.

Hanashi kata (Hah-nah-she kah-tah)

As noted above, *hanashi kata*, or the way one speaks—which includes vocabulary as well as the manner of delivery—plays an important role in Japan's etiquette system, particularly in semiformal and formal situations when various levels of *keigo*, or "polite language," are expected.

On such occasions, the minutely prescribed and stylized way of using Japanese has a number of aims: exalting superiors, flattering the other party, avoiding giving offense, maintaining and nurturing harmony, establishing social status—and at times, leaving the listener in the dark.

The ability to use *keigo* generally marks the user as being well educated and from a middle- or high-class family. It is valued as both a social and professional skill, and often contributes significantly to one's success. Young female employees of larger Japanese companies are usually given training in *hanashi kata* in order for them to respond properly to visitors and telephone calls.

Japanese sensitivity to "correct" speech forms, tone of voice, facial expression, and overall manner led to the development of precise guidelines for each factor. There is a specific *hanashi kata* for every situation that varies with the status of the individuals concerned—their sex, age, relationship to each other, and so on.

Some of the relationships that determine proper or acceptable *hanashi kata* are obvious (age differences, sex, etc.). Others are more subtle. In order to know the proper *hanashi kata* to use, it is necessary to know, or find out as quickly as you can without giving offense in the meantime, what your own status is in relation to the other person.

Exchanging name-cards among new business contacts is one of the key ways the Japanese identify each other's status. The need to determine the appropriate *hanashi kata* in a new relationship is one of the reasons why advance introductions are so important to the Japanese and why they go to such lengths to identify anyone who contacts them without a go-between.

Successful use of all the preceding kata is directly related to *hanashi kata*. In company and formal settings, it is almost always possible to distinguish between inferiors and superiors immediately by the language they use to each other. Relationships and behavior in these settings immediately suggest a very strict military situation involving officers and enlisted men.

How well a Japanese (or foreigner) knows and uses proper *hanashi kata* is another yardstick for measuring education, cultural accomplishment, social standing, character, and worth. Those who are especially skilled in this social art have an advantage and are generally envied and prized.

To achieve a marginally acceptable level of skill in *hanashi kata*, one must master the basic vocabulary and manners of *keigo*. There are several levels of politeness and subtlety within *keigo*. The very highest level of *keigo* is so esoteric that even few Japanese master it. It is practically another language.

As could be expected, there are also specific kata for preparing and delivering email messages and memos (*memo no tori kata* / may-moe no toe-ree kah-tah) and for making reports (*hokoku no shikata* / hoe-koe-kuu no she-kah-tah).

Tanomi kata (Tah-no-me-kah-tah)

Another very subtle but immensely important kata in the Japanese Way is the *tanomi kata* (tah-no-me kah-tah). *Tanomi* is derived from *tanomu* (tah-no-muu), which is defined in dictionary terms as "to ask for, request, beg." As usual, it has far broader and deeper cultural implications than just asking or begging for something.

The *tanomi kata* incorporates the concept of mutual dependence and mutual benefit in a give-and-take sense. It is routinely used in an institutionalized way in asking someone to do something special. It adds a very personal flavor to the request.

"*Tanomi*-ing" is, to put it in simple terms, asking someone to do something for you or help you achieve some goal when they can hardly refuse because they are in your debt, because you hold the key to their success or failure, because they want to build up obligation that they can collect on later, and so on. It is also common to *tanomu* someone who is in a position to help you and whom you believe or hope will help you because he likes you or because he is a magnanimous soul who will help anyone he feels is sincere and deserves help.

It is common practice for a boss to *tanomu* his employees when there is a crisis or deadline that has to be met and extraordinary effort is required. On such occasions, he will most likely say, *"Yoroshiku tanomu,"* which more or less means, "I ask you to please do whatever you can!"

Relationships and obligations bound up in the *tanomu* concept are an intimate part of the concept of *amae* (ah-my-eh), or the principle of indulgent love, which is the idealized foundation of Japanese society touched on earlier. A gung-ho type of personality in a Japanese company may take great delight in being asked to do something special or something especially difficult by a superior because it gives him a chance to show off his spirit and ability. If he fails, however, his reputation will suffer and he will lose status.

When male managers *tanomu* female employees, it is a different matter. It is more like an order phrased in a manner that suggests the women are full permanent members of the group, but in reality takes advantage of the inferior status of the women.

There are also casual uses of *tanomu* when people use the word to ask family or friends to do something like pick up a gift or remember to put the cat out.

Nemawashi (Nay-mah-wah-she)

Tanomu is closely related to the *nemawashi* (nay-mah-wah-she) system, or the behind-the-scenes lobbying the Japanese use in achieving consensus on important matters. The broad purpose of *nemawashi* is to create an intellectual and emotional environment in which everyone can willingly and energetically support a platform or project, greatly enhancing the prospects of success.

Nemawashi is also sometimes described as planting a seed, then unofficially and diplomatically nurturing it by subtle, persuasive techniques to win support for the project. In one form or another, *nemawashi* is the basis for decision-making in most Japanese companies—although a growing number of internationally oriented companies are in varying stages of adopting top-down decision-making to remain competitive in fast-moving domestic as well as foreign markets.

Risk Factors in Building Consensus

One of the reasons for the extraordinary stress in the Japanese way of doing things is the risk factor involved in associating with, communicating with, and involving your co-workers in the *nemawashi* process. If you misread someone's willingness to help you or leave out someone who feels he should have been brought into the process, or make any of a number of other miscues, you may suffer setbacks to varying degrees. In serious cases, the mistake can be fatal to your career with the company.

A typical example in a medium-sized company: The manager of a department is asked by the senior vice president to do the staff work for a major project. The manager does so, but limits his *nemawashi* to the vice president and other members of the firm who are directly involved in the project. When the project is completed, it goes to the president for review.

The president becomes very angry at the manager, and kills the project—not because he thought it was poorly done, but because he was not quietly (without the vice president knowing about it) brought into the *nemawashi* process by the manager. He accuses the manager of not knowing how to *nemawashi*. This leaves the manager with no future in the company, and he resigns shortly thereafter.

Because of the risk factor involved in using the *nemawashi* process, it has lost some of its luster among younger managers. They know that if they don't learn to use such tactics, however, their chances of succeeding over the long run in a company are reduced to near zero.

"The difficulty with *nemawashi* lobbying is that you never know if or when the seeds you are planting are going to sprout," said a manager. "It is a very subtle type of manipulation that depends on appealing to the self-interest of others, with a lot of give-and-take. It is the unseen foundation of business in Japan," he added.

There is also a risk factor involved in ordinary personal relationships within a given group. Everyone is always on the lookout for any aberration or deviation from the cultural norm of Japaneseness. You have to be very careful to avoid being trapped by what you say or do.

"Most Japanese do not know how to treat others as individuals, and measure everybody by their Japaneseness and the collective interests of the group," said one.

In personal and professional dealings within a Japanese company, it is always necessary to be aware of hidden meanings and agendas, since people are almost never fully open and candid with each other. Direct communication is seldom complete. Complained one bicultural manager: "Most conversations are just *keshiki* (kay-she-kee), or formality. You have to decode what the speaker really means."

Managing without Giving Orders

Aside from new employee orientation and any formal training systems to acquire skills, foreign employees of Japanese companies often complain that no one ever gives them orders or specific instructions about what they are supposed to do, leaving them feeling useless and frustrated.

The reason for this is directly linked to kata, to how the Japanese have traditionally been conditioned to teach and learn in business situations. This silent system is based on learning by first observing and listening to general comments and hints, then slowly beginning to do the simplest and most obvious things.

In other words, the ancient apprentice system. The third step is to slowly begin to take part in the endless round of discussions that characterize Japanese management, eventually becoming a participating member of the team and thereafter naturally absorbing the knowledge and direction you need.

This traditional type of "instruction" is literally known as *mi-narai* (me-nah-rye), or "learn by watching." While still common, it is coming under increasing criticism by younger people who say it wastes time, reinforces outdated methods of teaching needed skills, and emphasizes role behavior.

Managing without giving direct orders is called *meirei no shikata* (may-e-ray no she-kah-tah), or "way of giving orders." It does not consist of giving orders in the Western sense. It is creating a situation in which individual workers know what they are supposed to do, are given the necessary incentive to do it, and are rewarded when they do. The system is designed to avoid singling individuals out, to diffuse responsibility and to give each person the opportunity to do his or her best—always within the confines of the group and its interests.

What might be called a sub-division of these particular kata is *shiji no dashi kata* (she-jee no dah-shee kah-tah), or "way of giving direction," which follows the same guidelines and has the same goals.

There is also *meirei no ukekata*, or "how to receive/accept meirei"; this is an extension of the *meirei no shikata* concept that covers how employees are expected to react to it. The essence of *meirei no ukekata* is that employees are expected to carry out the wishes of management in a way that will please everyone and enhance the image/status of the group. This includes the idea that employees will use their own initiative, motivate themselves, and not let management or the group down.

In keeping with the group-oriented shame factor as a control mechanism in Japanese society, the most devastating way to get better performance by individuals is to point out the need for improvement in front of their colleagues. The power of this approach lies in the fact that because the individual's failings, which affect the whole group, are made public, then the individual has no other place to go, and thus becomes a target of pressure from his own co-workers.

The Japanese Way of Working

Most larger Japanese companies are microcosms of the kata system at work, with *shigoto no shikata* (she-go-toh no she-kah-tah), or "the way of working," playing a central role. Shigoto no shikata sounds simple enough, but it goes far beyond the obvious surface facets of technical ability and physical/mental performance. It encompasses the whole Japanese work ethic from groupism and harmony to the built-in compulsion for continuous improvement in the process.

Virtually every aspect of work in a Japanese company begins and ends with whatever group one belongs to. The groups are structured hierarchically as pyramids. Relationships within the groups are based on longevity and rank within the group, with these two factors often being synonymous with male employees.

In most cases, the lowest-ranking members of any group are usually the newest and youngest members of the group. In the past, women were included in this group, although significant gains have been made in terms of equality at the workplace. Japan still lags behind Western countries when it comes to having women in leadership positions. Some observers cite discrimination; others argue that the opportunities are there—given the existence of a legal framework and other measures—and that significant numbers of Japanese women, including members of the younger generation, are simply not interested in becoming career women.

That idea was supported by a poll in 2015 by the Ministry of Health, Labor and Welfare. About a third of young Japanese women had aspirations of getting married and becoming full-time housewives, according to the survey.

Only slightly more, 38 percent, said they did not want to dedicate their lives to being homemakers.

More and more women in larger Japanese companies have risen to become leaders of groups, sections or departments, but unless attitudes change, the numbers will still be lower than in Western nations and quite a few Asian ones as well.

The first priority in a group is the harmony, integrity, and survival of the group. The second priority is to achieve the goals set for the group and, if humanly possible, to overachieve them because the kata-ized system conditions people to regard anything less than maximum effort and maximum results as a shameful failure.

The concept of shigoto no shikata includes the state of mind of all the members of the group concerned, their attitudes about the company, their group and their work responsibilities, and how they behave in their personal relations within the group and toward outsiders. The concept covers what they say and how they say it. It requires them to take pride in their group and company, to be gracious and hospitable to clients and other visitors, and to go about their work in a warm, sincere, trusting, and positive manner.

The aim of shigoto no shikata is to create an environment in which the contribution of each member transcends the goal of just getting the work done.

Shigoto no shikata is permeated by two other concepts that are constantly on the lips of the Japanese: *ganbaru* (gahn-bah-rue) and *issho-kenmei yaru* (ee-show-ken-may-ee yah-rue). *Ganbaru* means to persevere and to never give up. *Issho-kenmei yaru* means to do one's best. When these concepts are energetically combined, it results in a high quality of effort and greatly enhances achievement.

Each person in a Japanese group is constantly monitored and evaluated by higher-ups on a subconscious and conscious level. The individual's mood, along with every comment and action, on both a personal and business basis, automatically "registers" on the shigoto no shikata scale of measuring people.

If the individual doesn't measure up in terms of putting the group first, maintaining harmony, and demonstrating a "fighting spirit" on behalf of the group and the company—no matter how hard he may actually work—he will invariably receive low marks that will eventually result in him being side-tracked off of the promotion escalator and out of the mainstream of management.

In such a system, it is virtually impossible for anyone to enter a group except at the bottom or at the top, and those who enter at the top are almost never fully accepted by those below them. If the newcomers are not extremely careful in dealing with the group, submerging most of their own personalities and individualistic tendencies, the group will reject them the same way the human body rejects the invasion of incompatible matter.

When the "foreign matter" introduced into a Japanese company group is indeed a foreigner, he or she is generally kept outside of the inner circle of the group, either as an accessory or as a temporary tool. If an effort is made to actually integrate the foreigner into the group, the situation becomes highly charged with all kinds of possibilities—most of which spell trouble for all those concerned.

In most cases, the concerned foreigner is not capable of blending into the group because he cannot speak Japanese at all or not well enough to eliminate all verbal communication barriers. Most foreign employees of Japanese companies are even less capable of communicating properly in non-verbal cultural terms. Their physical appearance alone is enough to set them apart as different, as not a homogenized, trustworthy, dependable segment of the same cultural cloth.

This means that the foreigner is a sidecar with a square wheel. How long he or she stays in the group, and how efficiently they function, is based on their ability to persevere in the face of unending visible/invisible barriers, how tolerant the Japanese members decide to be on their behalf, and if the foreigner is making a significant contribution to the goals of the group and these contributions are such that no Japanese can easily replace them.

On a personal basis, many Japanese are characteristically tolerant of the non-Japanese behavior of foreigners. In a work or professional group context, however, especially if there is even a hint of direct competition, the Japanese are more apt to take a highly intolerant stance and resist passively or aggressively, depending on the situation.

In Japanese companies, a primary criterion used by personnel officers when considering new employees (to bring in at the bottom) is whether or not they think the candidates can be psychologically molded to fit their shigoto no shikata.

The huge, multi-faceted Tokyu Corporation (railroads, hotels, resorts, restaurants, etc.) traditionally went well beyond carefully screening new employees. After they were hired, all employees—male, female, married, unmarried—were required to live in a dormitory for one year and work at menial jobs in one of the corporation's many divisions. They had to turn in weekly reports on their experiences and what they learned.

One of the goals of this program was to weld the employees into a cohesive group with the proper Tokyu spirit.

Fierce groupism in Japanese companies is one of the primary reasons why the head-hunting industry took so long to develop in Japan (although once it did, growth was explosive, as Japanese companies scrambled to find talent and expertise in a very tight and limited labor market), and why hostile takeovers of companies are rare.

Even friendly takeovers in Japan must contend with the groupism factor, sometimes until the original managers in the companies retire or die.

In the early years of the 21st century, scads of global investors found that out the hard way. This was a period when they naively saw Japan as fertile ground for hostile takeovers, due to such factors as dispersed stock ownership, depressed equity prices and liberalized regulations. They quickly discovered to their surprise that Japan Inc. wanted nothing to do with the investors and their deals. So what if stock holders could have made quick easy profits? Or if fresh capital may have helped invigorate moribund companies? The priority was maintaining harmony and ultimately the status quo. Indeed, the companies targeted were willing to put up a vigorous fight against the foreign "invaders" with the aim of packing them off home.

This attitude was significant given other events taking place at the time. Plenty of Japanese politicians, business executives, and academics had been busy trying to convince the world that Japan was finally shifting gears and leaving behind its post-war industrial model. Now, they said, the country was eager to embrace globalization and shareholder capitalism.

But the bulwarks erected against the foreign investors proved that plenty of holdouts from the old days were still instrumental in Japan Inc. The potential target companies have continued to hold on to their "poison pills"—measures aimed at fending off takeovers. Bloomberg News reported in mid-2015 that at least 20 percent of the firms in the Topix Index had such tools on hand.

Only five hostile takeovers, out of twenty-nine attempts, were successful in Japan from 2005 to 2015, according to Bloomberg.

The pre-1945 stories of how Japanese with anything other than straight black hair and purely Asian facial features were on the receiving end of severe discrimination would seem to be ancient history. However, these feelings, on a lesser but still significant scale, remain alive today among older Japanese. Many Japanese teachers take it upon themselves to continue this cultural bias in favor of absolute conformity, forcing their students to look and behave as much alike as possible.

Most of the young Japanese one sees in the trendy districts on weekends and holidays, those with their distinct and impeccable fashion sense, return to the traditional mold of sameness when they go to work on Monday mornings.

In theory, the conformity that is demanded within a Japanese group makes total equality an absolute. Everyone is not only supposed to think and act alike, they are also supposed to be equal in ability. Those who are more able than others are expected to behave as if they were no more talented than the next person. Any sign of superior ability is likely to provoke instant envy, resistance and, if the able person flaunts his ability, extreme hatred.

Examples of how this syndrome works, and how subtle it can be, are commonplace. For example, the recommendation of an individual for a special assignment in a Japanese company can set off a series of stressful, unhappy events. Instead of being grateful that his ability and loyalty have been recognized, the person is more likely to fear that being singled out from his colleagues may result in them turning against him.

Or he may become suspicious that he is being set up by someone who wants to eventually get rid of him. In any event, it is absolutely essential that he approach the assignment with the utmost humility, and painstakingly seek the understanding and approval of his co-workers.

It has been characteristic throughout much of Japan's history that the man of extraordinary talent and ambition did not rise to a leadership position because the group's equality-above-all-else syndrome resulted in him being ignored or ostracized. In fact, the tendency has been and still is, to a large degree, for the mediocre person to be chosen as a leader because they will not create envy or upset the group's wa. This is especially true in political and educational circles and within professional associations.

Historical exceptions to this pattern were common during periods of social upheaval and war, and are now becoming more common in business circles as the system evolves, particularly in companies that have globalized their operations and must now compete on an international basis.

On the home front as well, Japan's workforce has seen revolutionary changes in the 21st century. Japan has a two-tiered structure, with "regular workers" and contracted ones. The former are the legacy of postwar Japan. These are fully fledged workers at companies that include Japan's biggest and best-known employers such as Toyota and Sony. They are expected to remain with their company, if not for life, then for a long time. They receive a base salary along with regular bonuses, and a lot of other benefits like generous pensions and health insurance.

Their contracted counterparts, however, face a stark contrast in working conditions. Contracts last about a year, creating a significant amount of job insecurity. Pay is low, generating a new class of "working poor." Workers are typically compensated by each hour worked with no paid vacations, and they receive little to no benefits.

The media frequently reports on the unfairness of the situation: There are cases where contracted workers do the exact same job as regular workers, yet the former receives a fraction of the income.

The non-regulars accounted for 40 percent of the workforce, according to a 2015 survey by the Ministry of Health, Welfare and Labor. The fear is that the divide will intensify even more, as Japanese companies increasing make profitability (rather than workers' welfare) a priority.

The government recognizes this and has been urging employers to narrow the gap.

Japan's kata-ized conformity factor is naturally responsible for the follow-the-leader syndrome that still prevails throughout all levels of social and economic life. Examples of fads sweeping the country are legend.

Japanese and foreign marketers take regular advantage of the overwhelming desire of most Japanese to "keep up with the Suzuki's" in dress, sports gear, or whatever. Sales people know instinctively that if they can sell a product to a leading company, other companies will generally follow suit whether or not they need the item.

One foreign ice cream company used the follow-the-leader syndrome in the Japanese makeup to introduce its product into the market in a simple but very astute way. When the company opened its first shop in winter, it hired a large number of people every day for several days to form a line extending from the counter in the shop to well down the block. Seeing the long line, other people joined it in droves, making the new ice cream an extraordinary success in a short period of time.

The Dangers of Speaking English

Every foreign firm, joint venture, and foreign-affiliated firm in Japan has its fair share of *Eigo-ya* (Aa-ee-go-yah), which is a rather derogatory term for "English speakers." These people have traditionally been resented by other Japanese staff members who do not speak the language.

Still today, many non-English speakers resent the familiarity that develops between the *Eigo-ya* and the foreign staff. They resent the role played by the English speakers as interpreters and liaison between the foreigners and Japanese management. They perceive the *Eigo-ya* as being favored and privileged—and they generally are.

Japan's *Eigo-ya* are fully aware of the sensitivity of their position, and react to their situation in a variety of ways. Some of those who feel that the foreign side cannot do without them sometimes choose to take advantage of their power to lord it over their Japanese co-workers. Others go to extremes to maintain harmonious relations with their Japanese colleagues.

Eigo-ya who do try to maintain wa with their Japanese colleagues are often forced into being two-faced. Others choose to be two-faced. When they are talking to and interacting with the foreign side, they pretend to agree with them and support them. When they go back to the Japanese side, they criticize and laugh at the foreigners. *Eigo-ya* in this category often contrive to thwart the efforts of the foreign staff to prevent them from succeeding and eventually get them replaced by Japanese.

Employees of especially conservative Japanese companies who speak English with any degree of fluency often feel compelled to downplay their ability or conceal it entirely to avoid negative reactions of envy and resentment from their co-workers which can adversely affect their careers.

The position of Westernized/internationalized Japanese executives in Japan is often precarious to a degree that suggests paranoia among their 100 percent Japanese *Japanese* co-workers.

In foreign and foreign-affiliated companies in Japan, the scenario almost invariably follows a familiar pattern: The foreign side brings in a Western-educated Japanese executive, usually in a sales or marketing position. He immediately begins doing exactly what he was hired for—attempting to initiate an aggressive and positive approach to sales.

His problems with the Japanese staff also begin immediately. In addition to being resented for his Western education and intimate-appearing relationship with the foreign bosses, his independent-minded aggressiveness clashes head-on with the Japanese system of groupism and consensus building. When he tries to short-circuit the subtle time-consuming *nemawashi shikata*, or way of consensus building, he often seals his fate.

More aggressive members of the Japanese staff characteristically begin a covert campaign to oust him by not following through on his programs and otherwise sabotaging everything he tries to do. When it becomes obvious to the foreign managers that nothing is going to be accomplished as long as the Westernized Japanese remains in place—and they often blame him—they move him to a less sensitive position, transfer him to a branch or somewhere else, or fire him.

Coping with a Humble Mode

Japanese often appear as passive, naive, helpless, and sometimes simpleminded to uninitiated Westerners. This appearance seems to trigger an uncontrollable compulsion in many Westerners to "help" the humble, polite, and grateful-acting Japanese. In actuality, such behavior has traditionally been a cultural cloak that the Japanese wore to avoid appearing aggressive, capable, independent-minded, and individualistic—all of which were taboo in the Japanese context of things.

This facet of Japanese behavior remains a common characteristic, although it was once a growing movement among bureaucrats, businessmen and diplomats to learn how to communicate and negotiate aggressively in the Western manner. This movement "officially" began in the 1960s with the introduction of Dale Carnegie courses.

Efforts of the Japanese to wean themselves away from their traditional humble mode received an extraordinary boost in the early 1980s with the success of the Japanese-language edition of Lee Iacocca's autobiography. In the book, Iacocca credited a Dale Carnegie course with having contributed significantly to his own success, causing a rush among Japanese to enroll in the Carnegie courses. The training courses have continued to be popular.

The typically passive manner of most Japanese is not necessarily a contrived act deliberately designed to mislead Westerners. It is the way the Japanese are forced to behave to conform to their own social mores. At the same time, however, the Japanese are smart enough to have recognized long ago that their apparent polite passivity gives them a considerable edge when they are dealing with aggressive, forthright Westerners who are not familiar with their type of role playing.

Americans in particular seem to have an acute compulsion to fill every silence, every vacuum—to talk, talk, talk, and tell all. The Japanese, on the other hand, typically soak up everything that is loose and give nothing in return. A significant degree of Japan's success can be traced to this one cultural characteristic, which one Japanese commentator describes as a "black hole" syndrome.

Often, all the Japanese have to do when they want something from foreigners is bow, smile, sit back, and wait.

Kata-ized conditioning in the Japanese way makes it difficult and nearly impossible for Japanese businessmen to react immediately or quickly to new proposals and unexpected events. They have been trained to react in exactly the opposite manner—to say little or nothing upon first hearing a proposition; to take days, weeks or months to think about it and discuss it before coming to a consensus.

The IT industry, of course, doesn't operate by these rules, with its lightning-quick development schedules and intense demands to constantly innovate. And that probably explains why Japan missed the IT boat in the 1990s—and then had time to scramble to catch up.

Foreign businessmen who are not familiar with the traditional cultural pattern often react in the wrong way. A common scenario is for the foreign side to be filled with euphoria and excitement at how well they made their own presentation and how "great" the deal is, then be on the edge of their seats with expectation. When the Japanese do not respond quickly, the foreign side is first puzzled, then disappointed. Some foreigners become quite angry, blaming the Japanese for "leading them on."

In so many instances, the foreign side reveals all of its experience, insights, and technology up front and is left with no bargaining power and a strong feeling of frustration.

The most effective way to deal with Japanese businessmen without giving the store away in advance is to emphasize that you (or your company) can help them succeed and look good at the same time, and stop there, resisting your own impulse to bare all, and all efforts by the intensely inquisitive Japanese to ferret out every last piece of information.

Once you reveal the precise details of how you can benefit a Japanese company, your position is greatly weakened because it is their nature to absorb the message and reject the messenger. Another aspect of this characteristic behavior is that the concept of technology and experience having proprietary value was traditionally alien to the Japanese. Once a foreign company signs a contract with a Japanese firm, the tendency is for the Japanese side to presume that it can obtain any service, any information the foreign company possesses regardless of the limited nature of the contract. Summarily refusing to comply with such requests can seriously damage a relationship. It is necessary to explain very formally and diplomatically that such requests cost time and money and cannot be honored without a new understanding that details the additional fees to be paid.

Etiquette as a Weapon

Foreign business people visiting Japan on brief trips typically get a false impression of what they think they have accomplished. The full force of the courtesy kata of the Japanese system is always in play on first meetings. The visitor, especially if he represents a large, well-known company, usually gets royal treatment. Representatives of lesser firms as well are normally treated with a degree and quality of hospitality that is very seductive.

Personal attention, hospitality, and entertainment showered upon foreign visitors by the Japanese is invariably enough to soften them up. When this is combined with the Japanese custom of avoiding direct criticism, confrontation and clear-cut rejections, it becomes a formidable barrier to understanding. Not being familiar with the Japanese way and therefore unable to recognize Japanese reality, many visitors mislead themselves into believing that everything is going great, and that they are making progress.

Foreign businessmen taking up residence in Japan have important advantages over visitors on brief trips, but they too face similar problems until they learn how the drama of business is played by the Japanese. Even after the newcomers learn the system and get their own act down pat, however, they generally find that their efficiency drops off dramatically. It simply takes considerably longer to do things because of the Japanese Way.

Among other things, the typical foreign businessman in Japan cannot make his own phone calls unless he is calling someone who speaks English or some other foreign language.

Foreign visitors often require guides and interpreters to help them find the Japanese companies they want to visit.

During the drawn-out getting-acquainted process, the foreign businessman is expected to adhere closely to the kata-ized behavior patterns expected by the Japanese, including good-humored patience, responding energetically and thoroughly to what often seems to be an unending series of questions and requests for additional information, ceremonial politeness, sincerity, dependability, and so on.[6]

---

[6] See the author's *Businessman's Quick Guide to Japan* (Charles E. Tuttle/ Yen Books) and *Japanese Etiquette & Ethics in Business* (NTC Business Books/ McGraw-Hill).

Cultural gaps between Western and Japanese business ways that are encountered by bilingual and bicultural foreign consultants in Japan are especially revealing.

Said one: "When I was first retained by a major Japanese company, the people I was involved with treated me as an outsider because of my foreign face. But once they got to know me and recognized that I could communicate with them and that I wanted to help them solve their problems, they ostensibly accepted me as a member of their group, supported me in my research, and encouraged me to recommend new approaches. I was treated as a *meiyo Nihonjin* (may-ee-yoe Nee-hone-jean), or 'honorary Japanese.'"

"When I made my recommendations, however, they could not accept them and immediately reverted to treating me as an outsider. My status as an honorary Japanese lasted only as long as I did not represent a threat to their way of doing things."

This consultant said his thirty-five years in Japan had taught him that it is impossible for the Japanese to develop the kind of relationships with non-Japanese that they have with each other. "Total language and cultural fluency has nothing to do with it," he said. "Their cultural programming is simply too strong for them to overcome. Distrust of foreigners is too deeply ingrained in them."

A Tokyo-based logistics consultant tells a similar story. He recalls providing Japanese clients with detailed recommendations based on best practices and other industry norms and the opinions of experts—only to have the most basic advice picked apart piece by piece.

The frustrating part, he explained, is that the critics are not typically logistics experts themselves. Rather, they are "company people," who have been put in charge of the company's logistics operations after stints in other unrelated departments.

"I'm tired of being second guessed by a guy who had come from general affairs," he said.

At the same time, loyalty in Japan is a kata, not a universal principle. The Japanese are conditioned to be loyal to groups and to expect the same degree of loyalty in return. If a group fails to demonstrate the degree of loyalty they expect, they readily shift their allegiance.

To a fairly large extent, this attitude has given way in the face of the IT industry and changes dictated by the forces of globalization. Japanese companies, including the old and traditional ones, have been trying to come to terms with the new industrial and business order, which may seem colder and less personal than the old days.

Nowadays, people in Japanese business and industry have come to realize that doing work quickly and efficiently for foreign clients, often in the role of supplier, is par for the course.

The cultural exclusivity of the Japanese has another aspect that is the source of many of the problems and friction between them and non-Japanese. They unconsciously distinguish between communicating in the Japanese language and in foreign languages. Communication in English or other foreign languages is often not regarded as "official" or binding, as representing the real world.

This factor impacts on virtually all relations the Japanese have with non-Japanese. Most foreign businessmen attempting to deal with their Japanese counterparts are first handicapped because they cannot speak Japanese. They then bring in interpreters, who are usually Japanese, presuming this solves the communication problem, only to discover later that the Japanese understanding of the situation between the two parties is quite different. "What transpires in a foreign language is in another dimension," said a veteran consultant.

Another critical aspect of this common situation is that the English-speaking Japanese interpreter brought into the scenario is almost never the perfect conduit. He may understand and sympathize with the foreign side when speaking to them in English but he must also understand and sympathize with the Japanese side when speaking to them in Japanese. If he translates exactly what the foreign side says, in every cultural sense, he will likely offend or confuse the Japanese side. If he tries to convey the exact cultural flavor and meaning of the Japanese dialogue, it will invariably mislead the foreign side.

Avoiding Emotional Blocks

Japanese emotionalism, usually masked behind smiles and their stylized etiquette, can be a serious obstacle to establishing personal or business relationships with foreigners. If the outsider gets off on the wrong foot by being just a little too pushy, or by being impolite (by Japanese standards) in action or in tone of voice, it sets up an emotional block in the minds of the Japanese.

In addition, Japanese take business very seriously. Traditional companies, like banks and insurers, tend to follow traditional etiquette in their office behavior. Conversations are often made in hushed tones, giving their workplaces the atmosphere of library study halls.

Media and other companies are more open-minded when it comes to work-styles. Dress and attitude are more casual, little different from those found in Western and some Asian countries. The workaholic tendency from the old days still persists regardless of what sector the company is in, however.

Many foreign businessmen habitually use curse words and other forms of vulgar speech in their daily business conversations. Unless you know a Japanese intimately and know for certain that he accepts such behavior from you, this kind of speech is dangerous because it will almost always prejudice the Japanese against you.

Once an emotional barrier has been erected, for whatever reason, it is almost certain that the Japanese will not get involved with you even though they may continue a meeting or presentation for hours, and even agree to other meetings.

The right kata to take is the quiet, "modest interest," and "exemplary" behavior mode, while working to create confidence in you and your company. There is no viable way to speed up this process when you are in the position of seller or petitioner. If you have something the Japanese want and they are courting you, they will probably already have gone through their preliminary investigations and consensus-building routine, and may appear to be acting very swiftly.

As noted earlier, business relations in Japan are primarily personal relations, with a significant "give and take" element, especially in the sense of performing favors and repaying obligations. Individuals deliberately do favors for others, which include wining and dining them, giving them gifts and treating them to golf, etc., expecting that they will eventually be repaid in new business, more business or just continued business.

The Japanese press used to frequently report on exceptional cases in which a government office or company would spend hundreds of millions of yen in "entertainment" in an attempt to influence business decisions.

The Japanese are, of course, fully aware of what is going on when someone gives them gifts and treats them to more than casual hospitality, and they often make a point of returning the favors in kind in order to avoid incurring business obligations they don't want to, or can't, fulfill. This striving for a balance between favors and obligations is a delicate kata-ized factor in the Japanese business system.

Reciprocating favors is not always a balancing of accounts, however. It is also used as a sign that a business relationship is going to occur or is going well—a situation usually very obvious from the tone and mood of the individuals involved.

Wining and dining has toned down since the start of the post-bubble years from the 1990s onward. A huge scandal involving Foreign Ministry officials threw a lot of cold water on the practice. Then, as the country's public finances deteriorated, tax authorities imposed limits on the exemptions companies could claim for their entertainment expenses.

The Kata of Rank

In Japan's vertically structured hierarchical society rank has traditionally been a key factor in the kata-ization process, beginning with showing respect to parents, elders and superiors in behavior as well as language, distinguishing between the sexes, and following the precise etiquette expected in the various situations encountered on a regular basis.

To behave properly toward individual Japanese in the Japanese cultural environment, it is essential to know their rank in relation to your own.

During Japan's feudal age, social class could usually be discerned from wearing apparel and whether or not one was armed with two swords—one short and one long (the short sword was for use in close fighting and to commit suicide when this ritual was required).

Wearing apparel was just as kata-ized as behavior, and was prescribed by the shogunate government. The different categories of tradespeople wore similar outfits that clearly identified their profession and their social class. Only the ruling samurai class was permitted to wear certain types of robes, along with swords.

As with many other facets of Japan's kata-ized culture, the codifying of rank began in the Imperial Court. Prince Shotoku, who ruled as regent in the 7th century, was responsible for adopting the "Twelve Cap" Chinese system for grading and ranking members of the court and nobles. Each of the twelve different ranks was designated by the color and style of the headgear.

Clearly visible symbols of class or rank are no longer common in Japan. But rank, whether in the business world, politics or the professions, is still a vital factor in relationships. The Japanese remain very sensitive to class and rank, and behave accordingly.

As a general rule, Japanese do not expect foreigners to know and follow all aspects of Japanese etiquette, especially those having to do with rank. But the foreigner who does not know something about this factor in Japanese life and make use of it is handicapped in a variety of ways.

Among other things, ignorance of proper Japanese rank etiquette indelibly stamps the foreigner as an outsider—and ultimately substantiates the constant claim that foreigners have difficulty in Japan because they do not know and follow the system.

Sitting in the Right Place

No foreign businessman has been to Japan without experiencing the kata of seating. In keeping with their superior-inferior hierarchical ranking system, the Japanese are extremely sensitive to where people sit and automatically seat everyone according to their rank or status at the moment.

Formal seating kata in Japan also go back to the days of Prince Shotoku in the 7th century when he adopted the "Twelve Cap" Chinese system of designating ranks among courtiers. The Prince incorporated the Chinese court custom of seating people in a descending order from the immediate vicinity of the emperor outward and on successively lower levels. This custom, adapted to fit the circumstances, eventually permeated Japanese society.

In the Japanese context, as in other cultures, every room or space has a "head" or "power place" where the ranking individual normally sits or stands. Ranking guests are also commonly accorded this honor. The "power seat" is called *kami za* (kahme zah), or "upper seat" in Japanese. In a private Japanese-style home or a Japanese-style room in an inn or restaurant, the *kami za* (on the reed-mat floor) is the space nearest the *tokonoma* (toh-koe-no-mah), a "beauty alcove" used for the display of flower arrangements, scrolls, or other works of art.

In a Western-style room, business office, conference room, or hall, the head of the room where ranking people are seated is usually the farthest from the door and/or nearest the main window side. In a car, the kami za is the back seat behind the driver. In an elevator it is the center of the elevator in the back, away from the door.

Japanese are constantly guiding foreigners to the seat considered proper for their rank and status, sometimes physically propelling them when they show reluctance to go to the "head" table or the "power seat"—and when they demonstrate ignorance of the custom. Foreign businessmen dealing with Japanese should be equally sensitive to this seating shikata and follow it when they have Japanese guests.

Another important shikata in treating business visitors is to accompany them to the elevator if on an upper floor and to the door if on the first floor. Japanese hosts also push the elevator button as an additional courtesy.

Calling People Names

In keeping with the tiered ranking of individuals within Japanese society, titles became an integral part of the kata-ized culture. In private as well as public life, it eventually became more common to use titles than personal names.

Titles were based on official and professional rank and on occupation. When based on occupation, the titles often identified the trade—*Daiku-San* (dike-sahn) was Mr. Carpenter and *Omawari-San* (Oh-mah-wah-ree Sahn) was Mr. Policeman.

Titles are another facet of traditional Japanese culture that have stood the test of time and also the new waves of "internationalization" that began washing over the islands in 1945. The importance and use of titles is especially conspicuous in business, where, on managerial levels, they are routinely used instead of names. Instead of a section manager being Mr. Kato, this person is usually addressed as *Kacho* (Kahchoe), or "Section Manager," and so on up the middle management and executive ladder to the chairman of the board—who is referred to as *Kaicho* (Kiechoe).

Commented a young foreign businessman in Tokyo: "I learned the hard way that one calls a president of a company 'President Sato,' not 'Mr. Sato.'"

Exchanging Name-cards

Following the official end of Japan's feudal system in 1868, name-cards soon replaced apparel and other visible signs of rank. Because of the importance of rank, name-cards have continued to play a vital role in the country's formalized business world. It is often said, with a substantial amount of truth, that in Japan, if you do not have a name-card, you don't exist.

Of course, the exchanging of name-cards, called *meishi kokan* (may-she koe-kahn) in Japanese, is a stylized process. In the first place, it is "correct" for name-cards to be kept in a card case to prevent them from becoming soiled or worn. When introduced by someone else, the Japanese customarily face each other, exchange cards (purists hold their cards with both hands when proffering them), and say "My name is So & So" (even though the go-between has already announced the names), while handing their cards over.

They then glance quickly at the other person's company, title and name, and bow according to the degree of respect and honor the other person is entitled to while saying, "I'm pleased to meet you," or one of the other stock introductory greetings. You do not give your title when introducing yourself!

Once this ritual is over, it is customary for each person to again look at the other party's name-card, this time studying it more carefully to make sure of the individual's name, company, and title. If the individuals then sit down at a coffee table or conference table, the practice is to lay the other person's card on the table in front of you so you can glance at it during the conversation to remind yourself of the other person's name and title.

It's also considered extremely rude to fold another person's card, mark it, or put it in a trouser pocket.

From here, how the Japanese react to the new acquaintance, the language they use, and their physical behavior, is determined

It is often said, with a substantial amount of truth, that in Japan, if you do not have a name-card, often called a *meishi*, you simply don't exist.

to a major degree by the rank of the other person's company in the hierarchy of the business world, the person's rank within the company and the relations between the two companies.

The *meishi kokan* ceremony is simple in form, but it is important to do it right—to follow the right kata—if you want to impress the Japanese and develop a smooth, unstressed relationship with them.

Name-card exchanges at first meetings tell the recipients a great deal about each other, especially if both of the parties are Japanese since they can usually make an instant judgment about the relative rank and importance of the new acquaintance, based on the size of the other person's company and their position.

It is worthy of note, however, that when groups of people are involved in *meishi kokan* the proceedings generally lose a lot of their kata-ized formality. When one of the groups is foreign, the scene may take on the looks of a farce.

Fortunately, the protocol of name-card exchanges in general has become much more casual, particularly among Japanese who have become more global in their outlook and behavior.

The Structure of a Japanese Office

Japanese offices were traditionally drab-looking places, with uniform rows of gray metal desks and bare fluorescent light overhead. All of this has changed. Companies are nowadays more aware of ergonomics and how aesthetically pleasing and comfortable workspaces can lift workers' productivity and job satisfaction. Even so, the vast majority of offices are still open in style; cubicles are rare. Private offices are reserved for the highest levels of management.

Most companies adhere fully or in part to a system based on tradition designed to identify the rank of the staff, to facilitate communication (which is invariably verbal), and to maximize group oriented efficiency.

Office structure is based on *bu* (buu), or department, and

ka (kah), or sections within the department. The standard desk arrangement is very similar to a classroom, made up of several "grades" or sections. The department manager is at the head of the room, facing several rows of desks that are generally positioned back-to-back (so the occupants face each other), with a head desk at the top of the formation, facing the other desks.

Section managers sit at the head desk of the oblong-shaped formation, with a view of all of their staff. Their assistants normally sit at the first desk to their right. The rest of the line-up usually indicates the seniority of the individual members. The more senior the staff members, the closer they are to the manager. Newcomers generally start out at or near the bottom of the line-up.

This open-bay type of arrangement is typically Japanese in that the formation contributes to both the concept and the function of a team. Everybody can see what others are doing and can hear all conversations that take place within some distance from their desks. Foreigners who have worked in these section formations say that all the members have their antenna up at all times and that news of any kind sweeps over the whole office in waves.

Each section functions as a highly trained unit, very much like a football squad, with the exception that the section leader does not call out moves play-by-play. Projects are minutely discussed in advance and the process of implementing them is also carefully worked out beforehand, with each member on the team knowing his or her role. The manager is there to answer questions and make suggestions, but not to run a one-man show.

Section managers hold frequent consultations with their staffs, with one another and with department managers. Department managers are coaches who seldom go onto the playing field and may give only a few pep talks a year to the whole group.

Managers in most Japanese companies work their way up from the bottom, spending time in several different sections and departments, cementing relationships with their co-workers and gaining an overall view of the company's activities. Depending on the company, it takes from seven to nine years for a managerial candidate to rise to the rank of assistant section chief, sixteen years to become head of a section, and twenty-two to twenty-six years to become a department manager.

Some Japanese companies started experimenting with and then implementing merit-based employment systems a few years after the bursting of the financial bubble in early 1990s. These gave promotions and pay raises to employees based on their effectiveness on the job, as opposed to years on the job. This was and remains revolutionary stuff by Japanese standards. Early efforts often floundered and were abandoned, and the systems have yet to take root, if they ever do.

Even so, during the era of "Abenomics," the change came to be seen as part of much-needed reforms to make Japan more competitive in the global economy and help lift the slow-growth economy up to a sustained recovery path.

Except for the command function, Japanese company groups are similar to most military units, which are examples of kata-ization that are well known worldwide. Japanese company sections are the equivalent of military squads, which usually have eight to twelve members. Departments are the equivalent of companies made up of several squads.

In the Japanese system, a great many project proposals begin with section chiefs (squad leaders who are the equivalent of corporals or sergeants in smaller and medium-sized firms and lieutenants in larger companies) and work their way up through the chain to the executive level. Since the section chiefs are in the trenches and are expected to know more about what is going on than higher management, particularly when their project concerns a process, their proposals are often approved in part or in whole.

Dealing with the Consensus Kata

It is particularly important for the foreign businessman dealing with Japan to be totally familiar with the kata of decision-making in matters relating to external activities. It is typically a quasi-democratic process that involves anywhere from a few to dozens of people discussing a subject down to the bone and then coming to a consensus about what to do or not to do—this despite the growing influence of Western style decision-making in many Japanese companies.

Unlike typical Western executives who can make a variety of decisions on their own, the authority of most individual Japanese managers, including top executives, is still very limited. Most exceptions to this rule are found in companies where the founder is still serving as the chief executive officer, and in the overseas branches and subsidiaries of major corporations where decisions must be tailored to the local scene. As the still prevailing Japanese system of decision making on new projects involves many people, it generally cannot be done quickly.

Attempts to speed up the process by pressure from the outside may succeed temporarily but almost always back-fire in the long run because the pressure is resented and the decision may not be to the liking of people who are able to sabotage it.

Some critics of the Japanese system of decision-making say that Japanese decision makers, collectively speaking, are drilled in people analysis, not problem analysis, since their success depends more on their abilities to persuade or manipulate their colleagues than on defining problems and opportunities. This is no doubt true to a degree, but certainly not to the point that it prevents the Japanese from being very successful at solving problems.

The larger the Japanese company, the more "bottoms up" proposals presented by different departments. At any one time dozens of different proposals may be in competition with each other, which is another reason why it takes a relatively long time for a proposal to be approved or disapproved in a large Japanese company.

In some cases, there are several competing proposals for the same project. Often the best parts of all of the plans end up in one plan—a very effective method of improving the overall quality of planning but another time-consuming process that often frustrates outsiders.

"Foreign businessmen must not only learn how to nemawashi to succeed in Japan, they should also be aware that the process is frequently abused by many Japanese," an American businessman-writer in Tokyo warns.

He explains: "It is common for a person with whom you are doing business or trying to do business to make an appointment with you and ask if he can bring along someone else from his company. It often turns out that the only purpose of the second individual is to pick your brain. When you get such calls it is advisable to find out exactly who the other person is and why they want to meet you."

Brain-picking in Japan, as mentioned earlier, goes well beyond the nemawashi process. There appears to be a natural inclination in the Japanese to learn everything they can about everything—a trait that has contributed enormously to their extraordinary economic success.

Japanese businessmen and others ask questions and listen with an intensity, and to such lengths, that it often drives their foreign counterparts to distraction. When this cultural habit is combined with the tendency of Westerners, especially Americans, to automatically assume a teaching or lecturing manner in the presence of Japanese (and others), it gives the Japanese a double advantage.

Some Japanese companies still use the traditional *ringi sho* (reen-ghee show) system of writing out proposals and circulating them to all the people concerned, first on the middle management level, and then going up the ladder to top executives. If the document survives the scrutiny of middle- and upper-level managers, the CEO usually goes along with it.

When the *ringi sho* is used, nemawashi still takes place, with the document as the focus of the discussions. Authorized readers sign it if they are in agreement, thus diluting responsibility for any adverse consequences.

The custom has been adapted to modern times. For quite a few years, workers go through the process via email or shared online documents. The new media speeds up the process, which tends to be conducted more casually than in years past. Yet it remains a feature of the Japanese office.

Indeed, Google and other global IT companies offer services that promote the practice. It could be argued that it's common throughout the white-collar world to "share" materials online, so that everyone involved can put their two cents in, in a kind of *ringi* for the 21st century.

Still, younger members of Japanese companies are chafing under the old-school *nemawashi* system of decision-making. Some are aggressively pushing for changes that would allow them to participate more directly in decisions and to get individual recognition for their successful efforts. There is a lot of talk about such changes and how far they have already gone, but a significant portion of this impression is exaggerated, especially where major companies are concerned. Fast decisions made by individual managers in large firms are still rare at traditional companies.

Following the Chain of Command

In addition to the kata of appropriate manners and language, business and professional relationships in Japan have a strict protocol that is very similar to a rigid military code. One of the most important facets of this code is paying special attention to the chain of command and being careful not to get anyone's nose out of joint by going over their heads.

Just like a strictly run military outfit, the Japanese have been conditioned to expect everyone, insiders as well as outsiders, to follow the prescribed command chain in all relationships.

For example, if a New York businessman who personally knows the president of a Japanese company goes to Japan and visits the president without going through the firm's New York branch office, it is a breach of protocol that can be serious. The branch manager of the Japanese company will feel slighted and left out and will likely bear a grudge against the New York businessman from that point on.

Depending on the circumstances, the Japanese branch manager in New York may become suspicious of the motives of the foreign businessman and thereafter mistrust him. Proper protocol, even if you have known the president in Japan for years and don't know the branch manager at all, is to play it by the kata-ized rules of order. The Japanese are innately suspicious of anybody who does not conform to established patterns of behavior.

While all Japanese behavior is obviously not controlled or directed by kata as pervasive as those governing the practice of *karate-do*, Western businessmen should keep in mind that there is, however, a kata for every aspect of Japanese mentality and behavior, and that failure to recognize and take the appropriate kata into consideration creates discomfort and, if too pronounced, can doom any endeavor.

Another typical example: A group of Japanese businessmen come to New York to look into investment opportunities in the U.S. The New York branch of their bank in Japan provides them with a staff member to act as their interpreter at a meeting with a group of American businessmen.

Despite having been carefully briefed by a veteran Japanese consultant to keep their presentation general and give only an overview (with the details to be provided later in written form), the American side makes a profusely detailed, highly technical presentation that totally floors the interpreter and leaves the visiting Japanese delegation squirming in their seats with anger, embarrassment, and boredom.

The American side becomes increasingly and painfully aware that the interpreter is doing a very bad job and they become upset and angry that the bilingual Japanese consultant retained by their company doesn't jump in and take over the role of interpreter. The meeting is an unpleasant experience for everyone.

The Japanese consultant later explains to his American colleagues that the kata applying to the way the Japanese conduct interpersonal relations prevented him from stepping in and taking over. Everyone on the Japanese side would have been shamed. The Japanese employee would have lost face and standing with his bank's clients as well as with the American side in a way that would never be forgotten—or forgiven.

The visiting Japanese businessmen would have understood the presentation if the Japanese consultant had stepped in, but they too are bound by the dictates of the kata designed to maintain face and harmony, and the negative factors involved in the situation would have outweighed the benefits.

"It was an extremely painful situation for me," said the consultant. "I, more than anyone, could see that the meeting was going very badly, but I couldn't stop my American colleagues and say, 'Hey! You're making a big mistake! You're doing exactly the opposite of what I advised you to do!' And as a Japanese, I couldn't insult the Japanese group by behaving in a manner that would destroy my ability to work with them in the future."

Of course, this kind of cross-cultural encounter may appear silly and counter-productive to the logical-minded, rational-minded Westerner. The point is that the kata of Japan often negate logic, and that kata often cannot be ignored, regardless of how "dumb" they may appear to the outsider.

It is easy to explain intellectually the "Japanese way" to Westerners, including those who have had absolutely no experience with Japan. But it is virtually impossible to transfer full understanding and appreciation of such behavior to someone else. The understanding has to be emotional and psychical to really make sense and to be accepted. This means that it has to be absorbed in real life over a long period of time.

Western businessmen are constantly asking Japanese and others who are knowledgeable about Japan to tell them in a few minutes all they need to know to deal effectively with their Japanese counterparts. Such instant insights can help, but they can also be so superficial they do more harm than good.

In fact, much of the advice and counsel being given to Western politicians, diplomats, and businessmen about how to deal with the Japanese only covers the surface of things. It often becomes misleading because it creates false images and expectations that are not likely to materialize.

The recommended kata approach is to have expert counsel in all phases of a project/relationship throughout its lifetime and to follow advice when it comes from a genuine authority. When you do not have access to expert advice and must proceed without it, apologize (an acceptable kata) and do it your way, as diplomatically and as courteously as you know how.

Westerners interested in absorbing some of the philosophy and psychic conditioning that makes up the Japanese Way, without going to Japan, could consider taking up one or more of the country's martial arts, such as kendo and karate.

Behind-the-scenes Management

One of the most significant characteristics of Japanese management in larger companies/organizations, be they political, economic, or business-oriented, is that the people out in front—those who appear to be the leaders—generally have limited authority and often no power at all.

There are a number of factors involved in this way of doing things, including the well-established consensus process of decision-making that diffuses responsibility to the point that it disappears and generally precludes the possibility of one man running the show.

Often just as important as the consensus factor is the well-established Japanese penchant for controlling things from behind the scenes—a cultural device that has been sanctified over a thousand years of constant use. An early example comes from Emperor Shirakawa, who went into retirement in A.D. 1086, but continued to exercise power through fronts and agents.

Emperor Shirakawa was able to avoid the time and energy

consuming ceremonial aspects of power and management, giving himself a great deal more privacy and time to contemplate and maneuver. He could also manipulate people and events to a far greater extent than if he was required to do so publicly. He was finally able to avoid all responsibility for any of his plans or actions that failed.

With this Imperial precedent of *insei* (een-say-e), or "secret life," it gradually became commonplace for Japanese leaders in all areas of business and life to "retire" early while continuing to manage events from the "closet."

Unfortunately, there was a fatal weakness in this system of indirect management that contributed to Imperial power being totally usurped as early as 1185 by military dictators who, in turn, were to be plagued by the same custom for the next seven hundred years.

The *insei* system, only slightly modified, still exists in modern Japan and is particularly conspicuous in politics, where not one but several key figures control most power from behind the scenes, often with disastrous results, as witnessed by a number of scandals in the late 1980s.

One of the primary weaknesses of the *insei* system, as practiced in Japan today, is that it does not lend itself to a quick analysis and reaction to situations, and it does not permit effective power to be focused on specific problems. This puts the Japanese government at a serious disadvantage in today's fast-moving world, particularly where its international relations and international events are concerned.

While the *insei* system has been very detrimental to Japan because it hides and protects the sources of power from public scrutiny and responsibility, it nevertheless has been very effective as a short-term weapon against foreign interests in both the political and economic sphere.

Probably the most notorious historical example of the *insei* factor occurred during the mid-1800s, when the U.S. and other European nations began attempting to establish diplomatic and trade relations with Japan. It was years before Westerners realized that the emperor in Kyoto was powerless, and that the country was governed by a military dictatorship headquartered in Edo, as Tokyo was then called.

In a more modern context, the practice is anathema to the reformers who are calling for greater transparency through such means as a corporate governance and stewardship codes. Listed Japanese companies now, in their investor relations materials published in both Japanese and English, take extra efforts to spell out all the progress they've been making to maximize profits and shareholder value.

A great deal of time and effort was wasted in the 1800s because Westerners were not addressing the real power center. Even after the Edo-based shogunate government was identified, the problem of effective communication and negotiation was not resolved because authority and responsibility were so diffused.

This system allowed the Japanese government to delay its reaction to the foreign approaches and to design its eventual responses to suit its own purposes, not those of the foreign powers. This was to remain both the policy and the practice of the Japanese government as well as major business enterprises up to the present time.

Dealing with the Japanese government or a large commercial enterprise today is very much like trying to grasp the arms of an octopus that keeps itself surrounded by a semi-opaque cloud of cultural smoke.

Inter-company Relations

Inter-company relations in Japan are also kata-ized in keeping with the overall formal nature of traditional etiquette. Business between companies is not done on an ordinary company-to-company basis. It is primarily done on a people-to-people basis, meaning that personal and human relations have to be established with the right managers before a transaction can occur.

Although the stricter requirements for first establishing personal relations with new firms have diminished significantly in recent decades, it is still common for managers to refuse to do business with companies they would like to sell to or buy from because the "proper relationship" does not exist. The first challenge in doing business with any Japanese company is for middle- and upper-level managers to establish the necessary personal ties on which trust and confidence are based.

Establishing such relationships invariably requires numerous meetings inside and outside of the company, with eating and drinking together playing a key role in the process. In fact, Japanese businessmen generally do not feel comfortable with anyone until they have gotten "drunk" together—the rationale being that you cannot really get to know people until all their defenses and facades are down and their true "heart" is revealed.

Strict Japanese etiquette prevents this from happening except for during after-work drinking sessions. The first kata in approaching a Japanese company is to go in with an introduction, preferably from someone they know personally and respect, or are strongly obligated to—such as their banker, a key supplier or customer, etc. Introductions from government agencies also carry weight.

All of the other company-to-company kata involve one or more facets of the etiquette system—from exchanging namecards to making courtesy calls on special occasions (especially at the beginning of each new year), giving gifts when appropriate, and fulfilling a variety of social/personal obligations that come with building and sustaining the kind of relationship that is required in Japan to begin and to continue doing business.

Whether or not individuals or companies have established relationships generally determines the ethics of any contact between them. If there is no established relationship, there is no specific obligation to treat the other party fairly (in the Western sense). In other words, Japanese tend to be "fair" only to those with whom they have on-going, desirable relationships.

Since fairness in the form of equal treatment and equal opportunity for all is the bedrock of American ethics, Japanese and Americans often find themselves at loggerheads.

Foreign businessmen who expect to be treated fairly by Japanese companies without having established a good, working relationship in the beginning are more likely to be treated as adversaries.

The Advantages of Illogical Thinking

One of the most conspicuous characteristics of the Japanese Way is that they are conditioned to think in what can be described as circular/holistic terms, rather than in the narrow straight lines that the West favors. When viewed from the Western standpoint, Japanese thinking and behavior often seem irrational.

In reality, however, the Japanese way of thinking and acting just as often turns out to be more rational, more logical, than the Western way because the Japanese approach is often more comprehensive, since it takes illogical as well as contradictory factors into consideration.

The fact that the traditional cultural mind-set of the Japanese is based in a significant part on the ambiguities, as well as the seeming contradictions of life, has turned out to be one of their greatest strengths in dealing with the growing complexities of the modern world.

It would appear that one of the most conspicuous and vital advantages the ambiguity-minded Japanese have is their attitude and approach toward certain forms of IT. "Fuzzy logic" is one example of this.

Japanese were not the first to conceive and develop the concept of fuzzy logic in programming computers. That was primarily the work of American scientists, but the mainstream American and European computer scientists were philosophically opposed to "fuzzy thinking" and tended to ignore its validity and potential.

This cultural failure of the Western scientific community allowed Japanese scientists to become leaders in the practical application of holistic computer logic. By 1990, dozens of major Japanese companies (with government support) were using fuzzy logic to achieve far more precise and adaptable control of robots and a wide variety of household appliances and electronic equipment, from subway systems to air-conditioning, than their Western counterparts who were just beginning to catch up.

It was ironic that one of the kata-ized Japanese traits that had been most criticized by Westerners turned out to be one of Japan's strongest assets in competing with the rest of the world.

Designing as a Cultural Expression

From the 1890s to the 1960s, the Japanese were known to the West primarily as product copiers, a role that had been culturally required of them for nearly two thousand years. The kata of copying was transmitted to each new generation through a pervasive, long-term apprentice system that made each workman or craftsman a thorough professional in duplicating products and meeting quality standards that had been developed and mastered by past generations.

There was very little innovation or inventiveness in Japan during the long feudal period (1192–1868). In fact, the kata system worked against change, and the political system often made change undesirable if not illegal. Once Japan had achieved a minutely defined political, economic, and etiquette system, the culture became relatively static. The concept of *kaizen* (kighzen), or "continuous improvement," was a modern addition to the Japanese Way.

It was not until the 1950s that the Japanese became completely free to introduce *kaizen*—to utilize their skills in designing new products or redesigning old ones to suit their tastes. Freed from centuries of political, economic, and social repression, they brought an extraordinary amount of energy, direction and aesthetic ability to the challenge of designing new things. There were no taboos, no ingrained mental blocks, about how things should look, and some of their earliest designs—in shoes for example—were bizarre to Western eyes. But their culturally conditioned aesthetic sense and physical skills, plus their propensity to humanize ordinary utilitarian things, quickly came to the fore.

Within a decade, the Japanese were known worldwide for both the quality and design of their products. The special designing ability of the Japanese is also a product of their kata-ized culture, beginning with their writing system and including their handicrafts and their traditional formalized etiquette, all of which are learned and transmitted by specific kata.

The training that all Japanese receive as part of their basic education, and the feel for form and order they develop as part of becoming Japanese, gives them the sensitivity and many of the fundamental skills so important to the creation of products that are new, useful, and attractive.

Production as a Religious Experience

Japan's success in productivity is emblazoned on the skylines of the world and is visible in virtually every home on the planet. The reason why Japan has achieved such a high rate of productivity in such a short period of time (besides free access to the markets of the U.S. and Europe and other external factors such as other people's wars and short-sighted policies) is because of its kata-ized culture, including everything from the principles of wa and harmony, to groupism and self-sacrifice of the individual for the whole.

Japanese obsession with processes, their post-1950 "religion" of *kaizen*, or striving continuously to improve everything they make, and their equally powerful obsession to be number one in the world (because mastery is the ultimate purpose of every kata) fueled their spirit and their energy.

Packaging Makes Perfect

Outstanding design and productivity are not the only things that distinguish Japanese industry. Japanese packaging is also superior, and approached or equaled by only a few other countries. Reasons for this packaging superiority include their cultural emphasis on aesthetics and their skill in translating their highly refined sense of harmony and beauty into everything from boxes to wrapping paper.

Many of Japan's traditional forms of packaging—made of bamboo, other beautiful woods, or handmade paper—are themselves works of handicraft art.

Not surprisingly, the Japanese are just as discriminative about packaging as they are about the products they contain. Product packaging must not only be right, when it is sold it must be wrapped and tied in the right way to satisfy the innate expectations of the Japanese.

For a variety of things that are wrapped or enclosed, there is a specific kind of string or cord that is required. Substituting some other kind of string would not only be a glaring error, it would result in a strong emotional reaction from the recipient. If a high-end store committed such an oversight, its whole image would suffer.

Foreign businessmen trying to sell consumer products in Japan learn very quickly that packaging can be as important as the product, just as the presentation of food in Japan is given as much importance as taste.

Seeing Kata in Action

Visitors or new residents wanting to see one of the most impressive and important, demonstrations of kata in Japan have only to go a Mitsukoshi, Matsuzakaya, or Takashimaya department store (or any other leading department store) just before the opening hour of 10 a.m. and enter the store right as it opens.

At Mitsukoshi's Ginza branch in Tokyo, uniformed staff can be seen through the large plate-glass doors and windows making final preparations for the opening. At approximately one minute before the hour strikes, a braided rope is removed from the handles of the center doors. All of the doors have already been unlocked and the rope on the center door is just a sign that the store is not yet officially open.

Just before the rope is removed from the main doors, staff members take up positions to the sides of each of the half dozen doors and stand at attention, forming the kind of receiving line associated with very formal occasions. By coincidence, a huge clock on the tower of the Wako Department Store across the street begins tolling loudly ten seconds before the hour. There is a dramatic build-up. At exactly 10 a.m., in perfect timing with the tolling bell of the clock, the staff in the receiving line bow in unison as a signal that the waiting customers may enter.

All floor personnel, mostly attractive women, are at their stations, trimly uniformed and standing at attention. Managers are positioned at key areas on each floor. Additional staff, usually including the floor managers, are stationed at the escalator landings on each floor. All bow and call out in unison, *Irasshaimase!* (Ee-rah-shy-ee-mah-say!), or "Welcome!" to customers. Managers often also call out *Ohayo gozaimasu!* (Oh-hah-yoe go-zie-mahss), meaning "Good Morning."

It is an impressive example of the form and order—the kata—of the Japanese Way, and it is indicative of the care and thoroughness with which the Japanese do things. The kata visible in the department store radiate feelings of efficiency, confidence, trust, and security—all of which are part of the reason why most foreigners who visit Japan are so enamored of this aspect of the culture.

Just visiting a department store is often enough for first-time visitors to say, "Now I understand why the Japanese have been so successful!"

Many Japanese companies are even more representative of traditional kata-ized behavior in modern settings. Visiting

Konishi Sake Brewing Company in Itami (between Osaka and Kobe), makers of the famed Snow White brand of sake for fifteen generations, is like stepping back in time.

The public areas of the huge, traditionally styled headquarters building are furnished and decorated with impeccable aesthetic taste reflecting the arts and crafts of old Japan. Employees conduct themselves with ceremonial politeness, treating visitors with a refined etiquette that Westerners associate with old-style royalty. The atmosphere exudes competence, confidence, quality, and a serene wisdom.

A week after my visit to Konishi, I was greeted with exactly the same etiquette when visiting the corporate headquarters of Kikkoman, a Tokyo firm especially noted for its global policies and practices.

This would seem to indicate that there is indeed a movement in Japanese companies to rejuvenate (or resurrect) traditional kata-ized behavior among their employees.

One of the most conspicuous and impressive examples of the continuing efficiency of Japan's kata-ized system is the amazing promptness of its commuter and long-distance trains. The timing of the famed "bullet trains" in particular is as precise as a finely tuned watch—departing and arriving on the second.

This kind of compulsive attention and dedication to detail and efficiency are among the characteristic attributes that Japanese owe to the kata factor in their culture—and will be surely be missed if too many of the kata disappear.

5

Weaknesses of the Japanese System

The New Playing Field

JAPAN's remarkable kata culture has traditionally had its weaknesses as well as its strengths. As long as the country was isolated from the rest of the world, the inherent failings of the system were mostly kept submerged below the surface. Japanese were conditioned to accept the negative aspects of their behavior formulas, sacrificing their individuality and independence on the altar of harmony and the polity.

An American businessman who has lived in Japan for about fifty years, and is bilingual and bicultural, pinpointed one of the primary weaknesses of Japan's kata-ized system. He said: "In today's Japan, the playing field is changing constantly while the kata remain the same. In traditional, isolated Japan, the kata served as specific, absolute guidelines for all behavior. Now they are often a trap that regularly leads the Japanese over the edge."

He further commented that the Japanese turned kata-ized behavior into a ritual, and as a ritual it was unassailable. "How could a behavior be 'wrong' if it was sanctified ritual? To the Japanese of feudal Japan, and still to a considerable degree, life was ritual and ritual was life. That is the truest form of psychopathic behavior."

Donald Richie (d. 2013), the noted Japanologist and writer who lived in Japan for more than half a century, observed that "Japaneseness" is often a neurotic symptom.

Still today when their behavior is challenged the Japanese frequently say, in so many words, "Don't question our behavior. You are criticizing the rituals that make us what we are! You must understand and accept us the way we are!"

Asking and expecting the Japanese to change their cultural stripes does, of course, represent a threat to the things they hold most sacred and vital to their identity. However, they recognize that they must change and make much more of an effort to understand the rest of the world. This means they must repudiate some of their most cherished ways.

At the same time, most Japanese are not aware of why they do what they do, or what they might be missing because of conformity to the Japanese Way. Most of them are absorbed by their kata mentality and continue to emphasize its strong points as the ultimate social formula which the rest of the world should adopt.

Some of the most vehement Japanese criticism I have ever heard of the American way of doing things was couched in terms of kata—in this case, the fact that Americans have no discernible kata in much of their behavior.

But with growing exposure to other cultures, more and more Japanese are beginning to realize that they live in a kind of kata-ized fish bowl; that their society is ruled by form and formulas and in a sense, in many areas, is empty of the individual human content that makes up a much more complete and satisfying emotional and spiritual life. Such persons are beginning to question the traditional cultural values, and to break the molds of the past.

One way of grasping the ongoing importance and role of kata-ized attitudes and manners of most Japanese, however, is to view the overall system as a minutely detailed and pervasive religious cult in which both the thinking and behavior of the members are prescribed and the system—at least in formal and business situations—is enforced with military sternness.

While the feudal laws of Japan have long since disappeared and the cult-like behavior that was demanded of all Japanese is now far more relaxed, most Japanese continue to exhibit traditional values and behavior to a degree that distinguishes them from all other national groups.

Iki-kata (ee-kee-kah-tah), or "way of living," might have been called the master kata (or mother kata) of Japan in earlier times, when the way of living of each individual was clearly determined by social class, occupation and other specific factors.

Within these feudal categories, the way of living was basically prescribed and enforced by group consensus and peer pressure. as well as by law.

Japanese were programmed to know and follow the style of living that was established for their *bun* (boon), or their category and status. The various iki-kata that applied to them were not subject to individual interpretation, and remained virtually unchanged from one generation to the next.

Remnants of this cultural conditioning are readily discernible in Japan today. People are acutely sensitive about iki-kata—theirs as well as that of others—and continuously talking about it. Any member of a company or other group who lives in a way that is marked as different from the others endangers his or her standing with the group. It can be personally, as well as professionally, damaging to be conspicuously different from others in your own group.

Said one English-speaking Japanese female employee of a major company: "I am like an alien in a Japanese face who happens to speak Japanese. The people around me are always asking me why I am different. Why I speak English. Why I think and sometimes behave differently than what they do. It just drives them up the wall."

Conforming to the expected iki-kata is a serious strain on the Japanese because it is role-playing to an extreme degree. It is like living on a stage where one's performance is under constant surveillance, and any failure in form, dialogue, or tone of voice is seen as a serious character and personality weakness and being un-Japanese, and therefore unacceptable.

This factor is the source of a great deal of frustration and anguish in Japan today because more and more young people are attempting to express their own individuality, to deliberately be different from other people, especially the huge mass of stereotypical Japanese. As more of these young people succeed in breaking out of the iki-kata molds of the past, the less likely they will be to conform to other kata-ized facets of the Japanese system.

Disenchantment with the Japanese system goes beyond new-age teenagers. Labor Ministry statistics show that job-hopping among middle-aged men in major corporations, almost unheard of in the 1970s, is common. Dissatisfaction with work and a greater sense of personal freedom have turned job-hopping from taboo to trend, said a ministry spokesman back in 2001. Even more compelling than job-hopping is the growing number of Japanese men who drop out of sight each year because of alienation from the nation's workaholic culture and from their families.

While the kata factor has helped preserve and sustain some of the arts of traditional Japan, it has worked against the flowering of modern art where individual interpretation and flights of imagination are often keys to greatness.

Critics say that the art world in Japan is so rigid that it produces artists who are technically polished but lacking in emotion and fire. This has resulted in droves of young musicians and painters fleeing Japan and establishing colonies abroad.

Because the lifestyle of Japan's younger generations is undergoing profound changes, there is a conspicuous degree of apparent artificiality about much of the hybrid attitudes and forms that one now encounters. "Many people in Japan are no longer real," said one critic. "Japanese who speak English are faking it. Some of them cannot be real even in Japanese. They are faking it in both languages and cultures."

After Westerners began attaching growing significance to the distinctive Japanese Way of doing things, particularly from the early 1970s on, the Japanese themselves gradually picked up on the theme and soon became even more fascinated than Westerners with their cultural traits. This has led to a growing debate about whether or not Japan should give up its traditional culture in order to be more in tune with Western countries.

Right-brain vs. Left-brain Influences

Many theories have been put forth by Japanese psychologists, sociologists, businessmen, and others in an attempt to explain typical Japanese behavior and attitudes. They were particularly active during Japan's bubble era. The most unusual of these theories was one advanced by Dr. Tadanobu Tsunoda, formerly a lecturer in ontology and audiology at the Tokyo Medical and Dental University, and a professor at the Department of Auditory Disorders at the Medical Research Institute of TMDU.

Dr. Tsunoda, who published his theory in a book entitled *The Japanese Brain—Uniqueness and Universality*, presented data which he said proved that the Japanese use their brains differently than other people, and that this difference accounts for the uniqueness of the Japanese way of thinking and acting.

Dr. Tsunoda attributed the uniqueness of the Japanese to their language. He said the Japanese are "Japanese" because they speak the Japanese language, which is processed by the right side of the brain where the emotions are situated.

He believed that the prominence of vowels in the Japanese language causes the Japanese to perceive and interpret natural and man-made sounds with the right side of the brain, whereas English and most other languages are processed in the left side of the brain, resulting in fundamental differences in the way the Japanese think and behave.

He said this difference results in the Japanese generally not distinguishing between reason and emotion. He added that the only other people who think like the Japanese are the Polynesians, because their language is also rich in vowels.

Whether Dr. Tsunoda's theory that the nature of the Japanese language is responsible for the distinctive features of Japanese culture holds any truth, I fully agree with his premise that the language, when used in the Japanese way, influences the thoughts and behavior of the Japanese. This seems indisputable, and I have long used key Japanese words in attempting to explain Japanese attitudes and actions.

Dr. Tsunoda went beyond the idea of the language influencing the mental processes of the Japanese. He said that when the Japanese use or hear a foreign language, their brain shifts hemispheres, going from the right side, which he said is their normal operating mode, to the left side, because of basic differences in the sounds of the languages.

When this automatic shift occurs, according to his theory, the Japanese are no longer able to think like Japanese and suddenly find themselves in an alien world. Listening to and speaking a foreign language is thus a traumatic experience for the Japanese, he added, and the longer they remain in the left-brain (foreign) mode, the longer it takes for them to revert back to the Japanese mode and recover from the experience.

In hearing-and-brain-activity response tests conducted on himself, Dr. Tsunoda said it took him approximately seven days to return to normal after participating in an English language conference. He suggested that extensive exposure to foreign languages can befuddle the Japanese to such a degree that their right-brain hemisphere is short-circuited, preventing them from being able to think creatively.

But this is not always the case in practical application, since many of Japan's most creative thinkers and innovators speak some English and are regularly exposed to its sounds.

Whether Dr. Tsunoda's theory is right or wrong, it is in line with the observations of one foreign linguist, quoted earlier, who says that the Japanese have a tendency to regard what they say in English or any other foreign language as unreal, as having no bearing on what they really think or believe, thus rendering it to be completely unbinding.

This suggests that all of Japan's international affairs, be they diplomatic or related to business, should be conducted in the Japanese language, otherwise any true meeting of the minds is virtually impossible. The fact that most foreign dialogue with Japan is not and never has been conducted in Japanese suggests the immensity of the problem.

Doctors and marketers in Japan do attest that the Japanese read and process Kanji using the right side of their brains, whereas phonetic writing—such as English—is processed and stored in the left side of the brain. This is apparently the reason why the Japanese (and other Asians who use Kanji) have a greater ability to perceive and use symbols, which are now most commonly seen in advertising.

Much of the friction between Japan and the rest of the world is, of course, the result of inadequate and failed communications caused by the Japanese and foreign sides speaking on entirely different cultural frequencies.

The most common example of miscommunication between Japanese and foreigners results from the reluctance of the Japanese to say "no" clearly and unequivocally. There are various expressions that are commonly used to express the negative, but they mislead foreigners who fail to translate them properly.

Typically, when a Japanese says "I will think it over," they mean, "I'm not interested." When they say something is "difficult," they mean it cannot be done. When they say "I will do my best," they mean what you are asking for is impossible and you might as well forget it.

There is no doubt part of the many challenges facing the Japanese is the Japanese language itself and a general inability to communicate clearly and effectively to other people.

They know that they differ from other people in many cultural ways, and there is a strong cultural-driven compulsion to take pride and in these differences. Yet there is also a yearning, especially among the baby boomer generation to be "like" other national groups and to be accepted as "normal" by them.

The younger generation is a lot more aloof. Many aren't particularly interested in transcultural issues, and they are content remaining safe and comfortable in Japan.

Learning English well does, in fact, have a profound influence on the minds of the Japanese, allowing them to step outside of their cultural skin and communicate in a clear, unequivocal manner.

The Downside of Speaking Japanese

There is another aspect of foreign language communication in Japan that plays a significant role in relationships between foreigners and Japanese. It often happens that speaking Japanese well or fairly well can be more of a disadvantage than a help.

This situation occurs when the concerned Japanese react by treating the foreign speaker as a Japanese rather than as a foreigner, the point being that the Japanese tend to be more accommodating, hospitable, and lenient toward foreigners than they are to other Japanese.

Most foreigners in Japan pick up on this Japanese peculiarity very quickly, and some develop considerable skill at using it to their advantage. Some also use it as a rationale for not making any serious attempt to learn the Japanese language.

Says a bilingual foreign businessman, "Japanese is a 'loaded' language in the sense that when you speak it, you are expected to act Japanese. Therefore, when I want to be direct and demanding, I use English. I also find English useful when I want to make it difficult for the other party to make an excuse. When I want to be vague, I use Japanese. This has nothing to do with the nature of the language. The exact same logical thought can be constructed in Japanese and English in more or less the same number of words, but if delivered in Japanese it will sound more direct, and often rude."

There are apparently a number of reasons why the Japanese often react more positively to English than they do to their own language—even when their English is so poor that any conversation with them is awkward and frustrating. This response apparently derives from an overwhelming desire to practice their English, to demonstrate their international ability, or to accommodate the foreigner.

It is also common for the Japanese to automatically presume that foreigners do not speak Japanese and sometimes to ignore the fact when they do. Which of these reasons is paramount depends on the individual.

The traditional Japanese image of foreigners as not being able to speak Japanese, as outsiders who cannot come to know or become Japanese under any circumstances, and therefore as temporary visitors regardless of their status in Japan, results in them tending to regard all foreigners more or less as "guests." As guests, they are generally given special treatment.

Speaking English (or other foreign languages) helps keep foreigners in the "foreign guest" category and allows them to presume on the special treatment the Japanese typically lavish on visitors. Their mistakes and mishaps are commonly indulged to a remarkable degree, and individual Japanese will often go out of their way to help foreigners.

Allowing and/or encouraging the Japanese to speak English—even though you may speak their language—can go well beyond the guest treatment syndrome if you know what you are doing and can control the situation.

As Dr. Tsunoda says, Japanese think and behave differently when functioning in English. Their kata-ized ways do not carry over. The degree of the cultural change that occurs depends on the individual's ability in the foreign language as well as on his or her knowledge and experience with the foreign culture in general.

When foreigners communicate with the Japanese in English, the communication may be complete insofar as the individual Japanese is concerned. But how effective the English-speaking Japanese can be in communicating the same understanding to non-English-speaking co-workers or others is another matter.

Problems arise when the foreign side expects too much from English-speaking Japanese who have their own set of handicaps when communicating with other Japanese.

Generally speaking, the deliberate use of English to draw the Japanese out of their cultural shell and take advantage of the guest syndrome is usually effective in relatively minor situations where single individuals are concerned. But in important matters concerning several people, regardless of the subject, it is much more likely to be ineffective and dangerous, especially if only one or two on the Japanese side speak English.

The foreigner typically goes away thinking he has made his point and it has been accepted; the non-English-speaking Japanese is likely to be confused, frustrated, or antagonistic.

Speaking in Tongues

There is ample evidence that the Japanese feel handicapped by their own language, and have no compulsion about adopting words from other languages. At least a third of the words making up the language were imported from China ages ago.

Today, somewhere between 10 and 20 percent of the vocabulary used by the Japanese is "Japanized" English—English pronounced as if it were Japanese.

There is absolutely nothing sacred about the Japanese language. Since the 1960s, the younger generations have chopped, diced, and blended the language to fit their moods and the latest fads.

New words, usually adapted from English, are added almost daily—and usually make no sense at all to either Japanese or English speakers until they are broken down and carefully explained. The advertising industry also regularly introduces new made-up words.

The role and importance of new words in Japan is indicated by the annual "Japan New Words & Popular Words Awards," sponsored by the publishing firm Jiyu Kokumin-sha, publishers of the annual Basic Information and Current Technology Dictionary.

One of the more interesting winning words in the New Words division contest was *sekusharu harashimento*, pronounced "say-kuu-shah-rue hah-rah-she-mane-toe" (sexual harassment). My all-time favorite is *buru baado*, or "buu-rue bah-doe" (blue bird), a popular car model.

When this name was first introduced, one of my friends, who already knew what it meant, left me puzzled for hours, trying to figure out what it referred to. Another of my favorites is *kosu meto* (koe-sue may-toh), which means "course mate," and refers to female golf caddies.

Keeping up with the changing times in Japan is an unending language lesson that often amuses as well as befuddles.

The Japanese have become masters at using English words to communicate more effectively as well as to take some kind of advantage. It appears to be government policy that certain topics that are likely to be viewed negatively by the public are referred to in Japanized English words.

Channeling Competitive Power

Takeshi Ishida, a social scientist at the University of Tokyo, disagrees with Dr. Tsunoda's left–right brain theories about Japanese behavior. He attributes the distinctive behavior of the Japanese to "the integration of conformity and competition."

In his scenario, conformity of the highest order is achieved through the creation and maintenance of specific groups. Within each Japanese group, members compete fiercely against each other to continuously prove their loyalty to the group and to contribute to its growth, thereby making the group dynamic instead of static. Each group in turn competes just as fiercely against all other groups.

This competitive powered conformity not only generates amazing energy, as Professor Ishida says, it also makes it possible for the Japanese to effect abrupt changes in their attitudes and behavior because the moment a group demands a new attitude, competitive loyalty within the conformity-oriented group takes over and the members outdo themselves to conform to the new demands.

Professor Ishida notes, however, that there is both a positive and a negative side to Japan's competitive conformity within groups. On the positive side, the system provides for the resolution of inter-group friction and conflicts by compromise (because they threaten its existence), and it ensures that the group will act together as a single unit when threatened from the outside.

The major weakness of groups bound together by competitive loyalty, Professor Ishida eleborates, is that the system virtually eliminates the possibility of any member of the group taking individual responsibility of any kind. Another weakness is that once a group sets out on a particular course of action, it is extremely difficult to stop the action, even when it turns out to be wrong or detrimental to the group and the group becomes aware of it.

Professor Ishida says that the origin of the elements making up Japan's conformity in a closed in-group system can be traced directly to the village system that existed from earliest times. From the beginning of Japan's history, most of its villages existed in virtual isolation from each other because of the country's myriad mountain ranges and numerous political divisions. In the early 1600s, the newly established Tokugawa shogunate passed edicts forbidding residents from moving out of their villages, thus institutionalizing the closed in-groups that were already common to rural communities.

With the downfall of the Tokugawa regime in 1868, the new Meiji government continued to limit the movement of people from villages, apparently to prevent exposure to civil rights movements outside of the villages, and went to great lengths to adopt the in-group conformity and competition system of the villages in government on both a local and national level.

As the primary sponsor of the industrialization of Japan from 1868 on, the Meiji government strongly backed the concept of all companies also being managed as family or "village" enterprises in a system that was quickly institutionalized under rigid bureaucratic leadership. Smaller enterprises were operated very much like individual family units; larger companies like villages.

National conformity in Japan was strengthened by a universal education system that emphasized group spirit and harmony above all other considerations. Mass news media that appeared following the downfall of the Tokugawa shogunate became an additional force in homogenizing the Japanese mind-set in the values of the Japanese Way.

The only news readers got was what the media managers and government censors felt would protect and strengthen national goals. Given the nature of the traditional in-group values, the Japanese saw every outsider as a threat.

Since social and economic harmony was the primary aim of Japan's village group system, it was necessary to control competition by defining it in terms of the group. The only practical way this could be done was for competition to be expressed in terms of loyalty to the group. Each member was expected to do his best to prove his loyalty. In present-day Japan, this constant striving to prove loyalty incorporates the individual's immediate group, the company, and the nation.

Traditionally, success in Japan came primarily from proving one's group loyalty as opposed to individual accomplishment, and, by extension, from proving one's Japaneseness.

Japan on "Clark's Curve"

The most provocative theory advanced by Western scholars to explain the Japaneseness of the Japanese is probably former diplomat and university professor Gregory Clark's so-called "Clark's Curve."

Professor Clark said that the Japaneseness of the Japanese is directly attributable to the current stage of their psychological and intellectual development from emotional and instinctive principles to logical and rationalistic principles. Professor Clark relates this developmental process to instinctive values found in early village societies, and the gradual appearance of rational values as each society goes through successive stages of feudalism and industrialization.

He says Japan is well behind Europe, America, and the Middle East on this curve of economic and social progress, but that this is one of Japan's advantages.

On Dr. Clark's "curve," he shows Japan as approaching the peak of the arc, which he says represents the ideal between instinctive values and rational values. He says that Europe, America, and some other older countries are now on the down side of the curve, where motivations are primarily selfish and aimed at personal gain rather than achieving a mutually cooperative spirit and system that benefits all.

Dr. Clark's curve theory may provide a possible framework for understanding and measuring personal and social values in a society, but it does not answer the question of "what makes a Japanese?" or clearly explain the whys of specific Japanese attitudes and behavior.

All societies are no doubt somewhere on the Clark Curve, but none are, or have been, exactly like the Japanese, including Koreans and Chinese, whose values and customs most closely resemble those of Japan. The answer to the question, "What is a Japanese?" is both far more sophisticated and specific than where they may be on a logic-versus-instinct curve.

Still today the Japanese are forever asking foreigners if they don't believe that the Japanese are *hen* (hen), which means "strange," with decidedly negative connotations. I was asked this question dozens of times in 1949 when I first went to Japan, and I was asked the same question over four decades later while aboard a plane about to arrive in Los Angeles from Tokyo.

The last person to ask me if I thought the Japanese were *hen*, a thirty-year-old Tokyo businessman, struggled valiantly to find a word that would describe what the Japanese wanted to be like (instead of being the way they perceive themselves to be), and he finally said, "We want to be ... continental!"

This was the first time I had heard the yearning of the Japanese expressed in this term, and I was delighted with the sense and style of it. How absolutely appropriate, I thought.

All things considered, the Japanese are changing remarkably fast, especially so, given the scope, power, and ongoing exclusivity of their culture.

To a large extent, the changes are being dictated by the forces of globalization. They have been watching their Asian neighbors—China, South Korea, Singapore, among others—gleefully jump on the globalization wagon, and quickly become key players in the global economy.

In the postwar era, Japan strove to catch up to the West. Nowadays, it seems they are struggling to stay in a more competitive race in a crowded field of competitors. The news in 2010 that China had overtaken Japan to become the world's second-biggest economy had been predicted, but it came as a shock nonetheless. Many Japanese have since realized that adapting to—rather than resisting—the new global economic order is the most viable way of keeping their country relevant.

This will probably entail kata's influence ultimately weakening. The question is whether or not the people will be able to retain the national characteristics that have worked for the country, while at the same time abandon the ones whose usefulness has ended.

Waves in the World of Wa

Until the early 1990s, Japan's business world presented a facade of wa in excellent if not perfect working order. But in reality, even then, it often was quite different. In most companies, there were over-riding conflicts of interest among the section and department managers as each tried to outdo or outmaneuver the other to stay on the corporate escalator that carried them toward the limited number of top executive posts.

Competition for promotion to higher levels within a company often resulted in Machiavellian political intrigue that impacted on the attempts of outsiders to do business with these companies. Projects often failed, regardless of their merit, because of opposition from section or department managers seeking their own advantage or to block the advantage of someone else.

This political infighting within many Japanese companies, it sometimes being more intense today than in the past, follows patterns of kata set down generations ago. It is usually manifested in the behavior of groups, made up of either sections (*ka*) or departments (*bu*), that conspire to advance their own programs at the expense of others.

The kata-ized group system protects and sustains itself by acting more or less as a single-cell unit. The chief regularly takes credit for the brilliant ideas or accomplishments of underlings, knowing that he can maintain their loyalty and support because they are not likely to quit, cannot be promoted over him, and because they depend upon him to pull them along with him as he ascends the organizational ladder.

This system creates a facade of order and harmony that is often an illusion. In the past, it also contributed to the relative immobility of labor among Japan's top companies because it was virtually impossible for an individual to be accepted in a new group, except at the bottom when young and at the top when old. Just as in the military, there are a specific number of slots in a Japanese company or organizational group, each with its own ranking. No one wants to be shoved aside or pushed down by a newcomer.

Another key factor in the kata-ized mentality of Japanese management is intolerance toward anyone who does not play the game according to the system's rules. Deviations from the norm are not written down, but they become a permanent part of the individual's "record."

A manager who makes this kind of cultural mistake is typically shunted off of the promotion escalator, and thereafter is moved sideways instead of up. Until around the year 2000, one of the more egregious "mistakes" a manager could make in a tradition-bound Japanese company was to show too much independence and individuality, to achieve successes on his own and accept credit for them.

The "proper" way was for him to maintain a very humble manner and credit everyone except himself. Still today, the combination of exclusive group orientation and the vertical structure of traditional Japanese companies—the classic pyramid organization—often results in very poor communication between the departments within companies, inability to delegate authority, and very slow response times; all factors that foreign businessmen must contend with when dealing with Japanese firms.

The more globalized a Japanese company is, the more likely it is to have a so-called *bunchin* (boon-cheen), or "paper-weight" structure. The connotation here is that the organizational system of the *bunchin* company has been flattened (as paper is flattened by a paperweight) to make the flow of communication easier.

Japanese critics of the pyramid system of organization say such companies cannot convert to the *bunchin* system until they develop a clear philosophy and an equally clear company policy, learn how to delegate authority, and develop skills in communicating—all cultural factors that respond slowly to changing times.

Personal Failings

Viewed from the outside, older Japanese often appear to be caricatures of their culture; stick-figures who can think and behave only in one way—a way that was programmed into them from infancy by rote conditioning.

This impression is probably wrong as often as it is right, but the cultural programming still undergone by most Japanese makes it difficult, and sometimes impossible, for them to cope in a foreign environment. An arbitrary listing of the "typical" Japanese weaknesses the Japanese themselves often bring up include:

1. Inability to think and act independently;
2. Inability to take the lead in most situations;
3. A tendency to think in terms of absolute stereotypes;
4. Stereotyping everyone in terms of family, education, university, company, company-size, and position;
5. A tendency to maintain the status quo until pressured from the outside;
6. A tendency to do nothing rather than cause friction;
7. Withholding facts pertaining to a situation at hand;
8. Rarely saying what they really think;
9. Rarely volunteering a direct opinion;
10. Invoking their Japaneseness as justification for their attitudes and behavior;

11. Persistent small-mindedness;
12. Almost no sense of reciprocity in a general context;
13. Little regard for the privacy of others;
14. An undeveloped sense of the rights of others;
15. Inability to identify themselves with other nationalities and races;
16. A growing impulsiveness, impatience and rudeness, especially in Tokyo; and
17. Unrealistic arrogance.

Historically, the Japanese educational and industrial training processes were based on copying and learning by repetition. Subject matter in schools was the same for everyone up through high school. Students learned by repetitive memorization. Variations in the process were not permitted. This system created a passive population conditioned to follow customs and orders, and worked against change and innovation.

Basically, this traditional learning and training process continues in Japan today. It has weakened and is under heavy pressure to change further, but both the private and public lives of most Japanese remain in the grip of the kata system, and change—for good or bad—is slow.

Perhaps the biggest and most significant change in the system is that in some companies and organizations, group creativity has been given the highest possible priority, and individual creativity by maverick researchers and thinkers is now both tolerated and encouraged in some areas.

But much of this new freedom is generally allowed only outside the confines of the traditional company structure, in new semi-independent departments and subsidiaries.

Japan has scored well in recent years in terms of Nobel Prizes for scientific research. From 2010 to 2016, the country claimed eight laureates in physics, chemistry, and medicine, although some observers were quick to point out that many of the scientists were studying at institutions overseas.

Still, the kata-ized culture has given the Japanese a built-in reverence for rigidity that prevails in the face of all kinds of evidence that a flexible response would be more beneficial to them. This rigidity is still used for the sake of form and harmony.

Might is Right

Another value that became a part of the national consciousness of the Japanese following its opening to the West in 1868 was that "might is right," and that the domination of the weak by the strong is a natural organic process.

This philosophy had existed in Japan since ancient times, but it was given new life and scope by their observation of the Western colonial powers of the day and the importation of Darwin's theory of survival of the fittest.

Generally speaking, the Japanese have long felt superior to other people, although many post-bubble developments in the world have lead to a lot of self-doubt. They are still proud of their manufacturing industries, safe streets, and general honesty of their fellow citizens. But the Japanese media, as well as plenty of individuals, have also marveled at "China power" and the extraordinary economic strides made very quickly by the Vietnamese, Indians, Malaysians, and others.

Historically, the Japanese tended to believe it is right and proper for them to exercise dominion over such people; behavior and attitudes that have been present in Western societies as well. The sentiment more recently is to serve as a mentor providing assistance and guidance in economies that have been experiencing the kind of rapid economic development and growth Japan saw during the postwar years.

Another round of rapid changes in Japan are not likely to occur without effective, ongoing pressure from the outside. As previously mentioned, Japanese tend to have a deep-seated dislike, even contempt, for weakness. Conversely, they are impressed by strength, courage, strong will, and unswerving dedication to personal and national goals.

6

Can Japan Survive Without Kata?

Japan vs. the World

SIGNIFICANT advances have been made by most Japanese in broadening their traditional attitudes, but one still constantly hears, especially among businessmen and politicians, that all of the friction and conflicts between Japan and the rest of the world will disappear as soon as foreigners succeed in understanding the Japanese viewpoint.

Of course, the very clear message is that these problems stem from the ignorance and intransigence of the foreign side, not from the attitudes and actions of the Japanese.

Despite the fact that the Japanese are at least partially correct in their view of their international political, trade, and investment relations, cultural handicaps make it difficult and sometimes impossible for them to achieve the understanding and co-operation from foreign countries they so ardently desire.

Some of the handicaps holding the Japanese back are exacerbated by their kata-ized conditioning in the rightness and righteousness of the Japanese Way, in groupism, in consensus decision-making, and so on. This puts the Japanese in a classic bind. Their kata culture is the main source of both their most enviable strengths and their most debilitating weaknesses.

How the Japanese handle this immediate dilemma will decide their future for generations to come.

The Dwindling Kata

Learning how to read and draw Kanji, the Chinese characters with which the Japanese write their language, is no doubt one of the most important factors in the survival of Japan's traditional culture, but the overall influence of Kanji is eroding rapidly. The number of characters the Japanese are required to learn in school was reduced from around five thousand to just under two thousand in the 1950s.

The appearance of Japanese-language word processors and personal computers in the 1970s and 1980s contributed to a further erosion of the role of kaki-kata, or "way of writing," in the cultural conditioning of the Japanese.

As more and more people select Kanji on keyboards rather than writing it with a pen, the weaker the kata of writing will become. Even the beautiful art of *shodo* (calligraphy) seems destined to become a victim of technology. A "calligraphy machine"

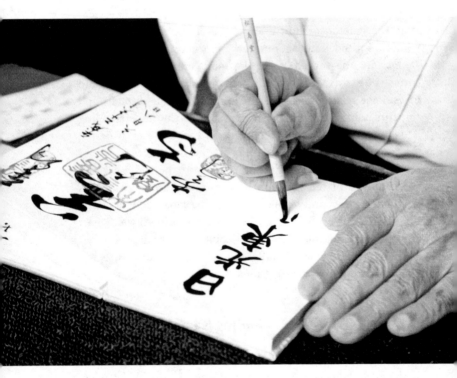

As more and more people select Kanji on their keyboards, rather than simply writing them with a pen, the weaker the kata applied to writing becomes.

called *fude gaki* (fuu-day gah-kee), or "brush writer," which makes it possible for anyone to mechanically print addresses and short messages in stylized brush strokes, was introduced in 1990.

Many high school graduates now have to take intensive refresher courses in reading and writing Kanji before they can hope to pass examinations that will permit them to enter universities. Within a few years after leaving school, a growing number of Japanese have forgotten how to write many of the less common Chinese characters, and some have forgotten how to read them as well.

The tendency for publishers to more and more use the simplified phonetic writing systems, *hiragana* and *katakana*, instead of the multi-stroke Kanji, is rapidly gaining ground.

In addition, voice-to-text apps that support spoken Japanese have been rolled out by the likes of Apple and Google, reducing the need to type or write. But for various reasons, this technology has failed to catch on in a big way in Japan, and many Japanese continue to text-message, even for long passages. Indeed, ever since mobile phones proliferated in the 1990s, the Japanese have become adroit phone-pad typists, banging away messages at lightning speed.

At any rate, in the same way that the introduction of streetcars and trains had a profound influence on the Japanese choice of wearing apparel, as well as their public behavior in the late 1800s, changes in the practice and use of Kanji today are inexorably changing Japan in subtle as well as conspicuous ways.

Just as the Japanese of the Meiji period could not freeze their stylized etiquette system within the type of constraints that existed during their earlier feudal era, present-day Japanese cannot prevent the further diminishing of their traditional way of writing.

Other kata as well are slowly but inexorably losing their power. More importantly, the very young are no longer being thoroughly conditioned in the traditional cultural molds in their homes. The result is a fundamental weakening of the famed "Japanese Way."

Usuda Tosen at an exhibition on contemporary Japanese calligraphy masters at Mao in Turin, Italy.

As earlier described in chapter 2, the Japanese style of wrestling, sumo, has long been an outstanding example of kata.

The national sport flourished in the 1980s, when wrestlers enjoyed the kind of celebrity status reserved for movie stars. But then followed a steady slide in popularity over the next couple of decades. The low point came in the 2010s, when the sumo world was hit with a serious image problem stemming from a range of scandals. The media reported on wrestlers smoking marijuana in their stables, betting on baseball games, and hazing their junior subordinates.

Things hardly improved later on. The public started hearing reports of bribes being paid, wrestlers throwing bouts, and dealings with mobsters.

In this backdrop, perhaps it came as no surprise to learn that fewer and fewer young Japanese had aspirations of becoming sumo stars. In 2012, the Japan Sumo Association reported the lowest number of applications on record of wrestler applicants: fifty-five

Clearly, young Japanese had become a lot less impressed with the sport and its highly kata-ized nature. The harsh, if not brutal, training and disciplined life in the confines of the stables proved to be a turnoff to the latest generation—and of course sumo's tarnished image hasn't helped in recruitment efforts.

On the other hand, the situation has opened the door to a new demographic: foreigners. The wrestlers from overseas have wasted no time in rising to some of the sports highest ranks in Japan, noted a March 2015 article in the *Economist* magazine. They tend to come from "poor countries with hard-scrabble backgrounds," the article said, and "have more drive to win" compared to their Japanese stablemates. The elaborate rituals and strict training, reflecting the thoroughly kata-ized approach, remain intact, but even so, they haven't prevented the sport from falling into scandal.

Japan is now experiencing the passing of its last fully kata-ized generation. Each year some 5 percent or so of the remaining "real" Japanese, those who were responsible for the country's rise to economic prominence, retire because of old age, or die off. Over half of them were gone by the year 2000, and all of them will have disappeared from the scene by the year 2030.

Furthermore, the first members of the "baby boom" generation, born from 1947 to 1949, retired in 2007.

The ongoing disappearance of present-day Japan's "founding fathers" and their replacement by people who are regarded as a "new breed," as virtual aliens, is viewed by many older Japanese as the most profound threat Japan has ever faced.

Fear of what could happen to a de-Japanized Japan is the main force in driving the older generation of Japanese to create one last miracle before they die: the globalization of Japanese culture and the economy.

Today's young Japanese, however, are less interested in the world beyond their nation's shores. A growing number are perfectly satisfied spending their time working and living in their comfort zone of Japan, rather than striking out for spells abroad.

"The hope for Japan to internationalize looked less likely than ever," opined an editorial in the *Japan Times* in June 2013, referring to a public opinion survey at the time. The Institute for a Global Society found that around a third of Japanese university students said they preferred not to become "an active person in a global society," and 40 percent of high school students gave the same response.

That attitude is reflected in hard statistics. The number of Japanese studying overseas declined 11 percent in 2008 from the previous year to 67,000, according to the Ministry of Education and Science. The downtrend was the mirror opposite to the growing number of international students throughout the world, especially ones from Asia. This is a case where Japan is clearly out of step with the rest of the globe.

Their youngsters' parents were a markedly different breed. In the 1970s and '80s, "internationalization" was the keyword, and young people who could communicate effectively in foreign languages and get around in other countries were envied, seen as the ultimate form of coolness.

The parents have since become company managers and senior government officials. And the generation comprised of their apathetic kids doesn't bode well for Japan, as it tries to make it in an increasingly globalized world.

But things may not all be doom and gloom for Japan. Many Japanese, including those of the younger generation, are fiercely proud of their *monozukuri*. This word literally means "making things," and it's often simply translated as "manufacturing." But the real meaning is deeper, encompassing the concept of a dedication to craftsmanship for the sake of producing goods of extremely high quality. Naturally, *monozukuri* could never happen without kata.

Rather than being sidelined or abandoned in an age of globalization, *monozukuri* has grown to become an even bigger phenomenon in Japan. Indeed, this quintessentially Japanese concept appears to be a reaction against global trends in industrialization. While multinational corporations in emerging economies churn out vast volumes of goods for masses of consumers in Bangalore, Birmingham, or Bangkok, some Japanese workers are carefully crafting extremely high-quality and high-value goods for smaller numbers of discriminating customers.

The products cover nearly every category: satellite components, musical instruments, brushes for applying cosmetics, you name it. What they all have in common is their astonishingly high quality. Many are also produced in small factories, fulfilling demand for niche markets. Many of Japan's largest manufacturers claim to be part of this heritage.

TV variety programs produce scads of gushing reports about how *monozukuri* is alive and well and helping define Japan in the 21st century.

Whether this is true is a matter of debate. A cynical observer might connect this trend to the goal shared by the government and private sector to avoid mass layoffs at any cost. Having people laboring away in small factories—even money-losing ones— is seen as a much better option than having them sit around unemployed. The media reports rarely mention whether the small-scale operations are actually profitable or whether they're receiving generous subsidies.

Nonetheless, the monozukuri phenomenon is evidence that kata is not just surviving, but widely admired.

Influence from Abroad

The biggest immediate threat to Japan's overall kata culture is, of course, the influence of Western ideas and customs, along with other trends arriving from overseas. With time and distance virtually eliminated by technology and their national borders open to two-way travel and trade, the Japanese are being directly exposed to the world like never before.

But they do not have an effective kata for handling this experience and are in a constant state of agitation. Western influence washing over Japan is especially disruptive because it emphasizes individuality and personal responsibility.

Westerners tend to accept individual responsibility and are more willing to take chances. Japanese society has traditionally spread responsibility within groups and cushioned the effects of failure. The Japanese are thus more wary of unpredictability and accepting responsibility than they are of failure.

Fear of unpredictability in Japan was, and still is, enormously strengthened by the power and influence of the kata. The smooth working of Japanese society is based on everyone following the accepted kata, as opposed to abstract principles that are always open to various interpretations. The subversion or flouting of proper form is therefore much more threatening to the Japanese than failing in any enterprise.

The ways of Westerners and other Asians, and their respective ways, represent unpredictability to the Japanese. One of the major challenges now facing the Japanese, as the old kata-based culture weakens, is to develop a tolerance for unpredictability and the ability to deal with it. This, of course, is much easier said than done, and it will probably be two or three generations before it becomes a significant part of the Japanese character—assuming they make the effort in the first place.

In one area at least, it's not a matter of choice. An explosion in the number of tourists from overseas has meant the Japanese have been finding themselves in ever closer proximity with foreigners. The inbound "tourism boom" came in the wake of several promotional initiatives the government launched from around 2010.

Previously, global tourism had largely given Japan a miss. Apart from being prohibitively expensive, the country was a place of language and many other barriers.

The initiatives, including such things as relaxing visa requirements for Mainland Chinese, aimed to reverse that, and the efforts clearly impressed people overseas. The number of tourist arrivals shot up, and now you're likely to spot more foreigners than local folks at popular sightseeing spots, such as the Meiji Shrine or Ginza.

The influx isn't limited to the cities. Foreigners are discovering Japan's rural retreats, like hot spring resorts nestled in mountain valleys or ski resorts in the Japanese Alps in Nagano Prefecture.

The influx has had an enormous economic impact. Government reports on GDP numbers routinely assess the effects of "inbound consumption," alongside capital investment, machinery orders, and other key data.

This heavy presence of tourists is not without controversy. Japanese hospitality has long been famous for being warm and attentive. But that reputation was created when foreigners were scarce. Now that they've become a common sight, less cheery attitudes have emerged.

When the influx started to gather steam, daytime TV programs got into the habit of airing reports on certain annoying characteristics displayed by the foreign visitors. The shows highlighted the "cultural differences"—to put it mildly. The tourists, usually from Mainland China, were shown littering in temple precincts, venturing onto railway tracks for photos ops, and pushing and shoving while inside normally staid Ginza boutiques.

"Selfie sticks," which never caught on in Japan as extensively as elsewhere, are portrayed by the media as a social ill.

What is more, the Japanese government has been promoting the country's regional areas as destinations. The target numbers, including 40 million arrivals a year by 2020, when Tokyo hosts the Olympic Games, suggest that no matter where one goes in Japan, groups of foreigners will not be far away.

As Japan's kata culture weakens, the incidences of intimidation, assault, battery, and other forms of violence are becoming more and more commonplace. Genuine wa is already hard to find in the urban areas of the country.

The Japanese are acutely aware that their kata-ized culture has broken up. They understand the universal principle that progress only comes with change. But, unlike earlier historical occasions when great changes occurred, they are no longer able to control events from the top.

For a preview of what one side of Japan could be like without kata, all one has to do is turn on the TV and watch a number of the regular comedy shows. In the 1980s, veteran journalist Ronald E. Yates described this facet of Japanese television as "the Kabuki-cho of Japan."

Kabuki-cho is a district in West Tokyo that is notorious as the sleaze capital of the country. Yates was referring to the fact that several of the most popular of these shows are in turn vulgar, irreverent, pornographic, thoughtless, callous, and even cruel. The shows are immensely popular, apparently because the comedians break every kata-ized taboo in the system, thereby providing a vicarious release for their audiences.

Because they are no longer able to prevent changes in their social system and are no longer in full control of their economic system, the Japanese may very well be unable to survive at the present level or higher without their kata-ized population.

Kabuki-cho is an entertainment and red-light district in Tokyo, Japan. Named after an unbuilt kabuki theater, it hosts thousands of nightclubs and hostess bars.

What the diminishing of the Kanji system alone means to Japan's future is, of course, open to conjecture, but there is no doubt that it will be a major factor in the de-traditionalizing of the culture and subsequently have a negative effect on the character and behavior as well as the abilities of the Japanese.

Kabuki is a good example of the ultimate in kata-izing human behavior, revealing not only its strengths in providing precise guidelines for each new performer to master the set form, but also the weakness and inhumanity of the system as well in that it rejects any individuality or new intelligence and thus stifles change and growth of the person and the art.

Still, the Japanese tend to look upon kabuki as representative of the best of traditional Japan, and continue to herd foreign visitors to the Kabuki-za for a taste of the "real Japan" without realizing that they might also be showing the worst side of Japanese culture.

To the degree that an automated kind of behavior served Japan's needs, kata-ization was a remarkable way to mobilize energy and skill in achieving specific set goals. But in those areas where flexibility, spontaneity, and art must be one, the negative effects of some kata, when carried to the ultimate, are equally obvious—and frightening.

Overall, the kata system will probably continue to be the most significant cultural influence in shaping the national character of the Japan throughout the first quarter of the 21st century. It will be carried forward not only by their spoken and written language, but also by their daily etiquette, their aesthetic, their martial arts, and the prevailing educational and business systems.

Japan's educational system and its employment and management practices remain key factors in helping to sustain the traditional aspects of the culture—in direct opposition to other efforts to internationalize the country. Still today one of the

The Kabuki-za Theater located in Higashi Ginza in Tokyo, Japan. Kabuki-za is Japan's most famous Kabuki theater.

most common sights in elementary schools in Japan is groups of young children, down on the floor, painting huge Kanji characters on large sheets of paper.

Many managers in larger Japanese companies are also deliberately trying to keep the kata culture alive because they recognize that despite its drawbacks it has been a key factor in the economic success of the country. But both the educational and traditional management systems of Japan are under increasing pressure to change.

There is no doubt that as the forces of globalization affect Japanese businesses and the people working in them, the kata system will weaken as a result. The more the Japanese give up the cultural practices that made them a special and formidable nation, the more of these special characteristics they will lose.

The price the Japanese must pay to globalize their society—in other words, become less Japanese and more like citizens of the world—is high, and there are many who feel it would not be worth it. Ideally, of course, the best solution would be for the Japanese to maintain the kata that are positive and result in desirable attitudes and habits, and drop those that have proven to be harmful.

In any event, it is too early to begin counting Japan out. The late Jean Pearce noted (just as American mariner Henry Holmes did in the mid-1800s) that the Japanese are still capable of surprising the world.

In a mid-1980s "Getting Things Done" column, Pearce presented a list of changes that occurred in Japan in the previous five years that were hardly imaginable a decade earlier. These changes included Japanese attitudes and policies regarding conservation, recycling paper, banning the ivory trade, and preserving the environment in general.

Just as important, such changes in Japan are not the result of a totally new awareness. As Pearce also observed, more often than not, they are a return to traditional values that were a fundamental part of Japanese culture for more than a thousand years. These old, familiar, resurrected traditions, like their kata heritage from the past, now constitute cultural advantages that have contributed to Japan's role as a world power.

But it was not until the 1980s that Japanese business and government leaders began to systematically sponsor the export of Japanese culture on a large, coordinated scale. The effort has only expanded, as seen in the "Cool Japan" campaign, an initiative of the Japanese government to promote modern culture forms such as anime (Japanese animation), manga, and J-pop music to the rest of the world.

This effort has been somewhat successful, based not so much on Japan's skill in exporting, but on the growing motivation of some people overseas to be receptive to Japanese ideas and processes, not to mention the growing number of people who have visited Japan as tourists and became quite familiar with the culture, ancient and modern alike.

Japan also continues to promote some aspects of its business culture. The country was long ago held up as a model of industrial development for emerging countries, especially ones in Asia, to follow. But the bursting of Japan's bubble together with a tsunami of globalization during the subsequent years shoved Japan the mentor into the shadows. Multinational corporations based in developed countries poured capital into China, Vietnam, Indonesia and a slew of other countries, quickly raising GDP growth and living standards. It almost seemed too easy. The Japanese approach to industrial development, which stresses harmony among stakeholders, loyalty, discipline, and a certain amount of sacrifice, suddenly didn't seem so appealing to the developing world, for which the benefits of economic success couldn't come soon enough.

Still, the Japanese model hasn't been totally abandoned. One element of the Japanese Way is still praised and practiced by businesses throughout the world: *kaizen.*

As explained earlier in this book, the word means "improvement" in Japanese, but in the context of manufacturing and other areas of business, it refers to a specific approach and attitude aimed at making continuous improvements. This means having

ALL employees—be they company presidents or assembly line workers—involved in the process and that they play an essential role in processes.

The Japan International Cooperation Agency (JICA), the government's huge coordinator of overseas development assistance, is a major conduit through which *kaizen* is exported around the globe. The agency sponsors workshops at home and abroad, usually attended by business and government people from developing countries.

In May 2013, for example, JICA announced a "series of Africa *kaizen* events."

Naturally, *kaizen*—which stresses close attention to detail and perseverance to achieve goals—draws deeply on the principles of kata, and could only have originated in kata-ized Japan.

From No. 2 to No. 3

One of the kata-bound cultural forces that used to drive the Japanese is the need to excel in everything—to do things better and to achieve more than other people.

The drive was particularly intense during the postwar years. Since the popping of the financial bubble, which led to a decline in Japan's economic standing in the world, this characteristic has faded significantly.

Even so, the Japanese are still intent on winning and being successful, particular when it's on the international stage. Whenever a Japanese person is awarded a Nobel Prize, the media goes into a frenzy. The dailies rush out "extra" editions that are handed out to commuters. The news programs on TV cancel or scale back nearly all their unrelated stories to make time for extensive coverage, interviewing the winner's colleagues and even old school teachers.

A stream of Japanese professional baseball players started entering the U.S. major leagues in the mid-1990s. American sports journalists are often amused by how the media boxes at parks are crowded with Japanese reporters if a player from their country is on the roster. But if the player is taken out of the game midway through, they promptly pack up their equipment and head home. The game itself isn't so important; the fact a Japanese person is competing against foreigners is what counts. When Japanese athletes compete internationally, the hometown crowds cheering them on often have zero knowledge or interest in the sport. Their sole concern is the Japanese player (or players) taking part.

That was the case in 2006, when the Japanese women's curling team turned in a strong performance during the Winter Olympics in Turin, Italy. The young women became instant celebrities and the sport of curling quickly went from being a rather esoteric endeavor to something of a boom.

The origin of the drive to succeed and celebrate those who do succeed is no doubt the perfection demanded by every kata in Japan's cultural system. Kata goals are unbounded, and carry over into all areas of life. Thus kata-ized Japanese cannot be satisfied with being anything but—in their own minds, at least—first or best.

By the 1980s, some Japanese began speculating that not only could Japan become the world's top economic power, there was, in fact, a good chance that it would—as much by default as by its own efforts.

But growing indications that Japan might indeed become No. 1 in the world were frightening to most Japanese. They believed such success would turn the world against them and they would once again be isolated. Even the most passionate expansionists were acutely aware that it was "too early" for them to openly seek the primary leadership role in the world. They need not worry now, given Japan's relegation to third place in the global standings in terms of economy size, its dwindling population and other indicators of a slow yet steady decline.

Japan's big-bang economy suddenly stopped expanding in 1990. The ever-growing "bubble" had begun to leak. Not only was the solid phalanx they presented to themselves and the world an illusion, the world had changed, and even the most admirable of their kata were not enough for them to overcome the weakness of their way, and the new economic forces roiling the world at large.

Japan Today

Japan has had its time in the sun, and is positioning itself to once again play second fiddle to China, the U.S., and eventually other countries as well. But the country remains rich in human resources and technical capital, and will continue to play a leading role in the world economy, offering opportunities to foreign companies.

The weakening of the kata culture, together with the harsh realities of globalization for "Japan Inc." and the country's demographic squeeze, have worked to lower Japan's business and cultural defenses. It used to take intimate familiarity with the system, obstinate persistence and a lot of patience to penetrate it, and in some cases it still does. True, Japan remains a harder nut to crack than Singapore or Hong Kong for most multinational companies, but foreign people and firms have managed to forge close and lucrative partnerships with some of Japan's biggest and most influential companies.

Boeing is a case in point. Its 787 Dreamliner was hailed as the future of aviation when first rolled out. About a third of this airliner, including its most technologically sophisticated components, was built by Japanese suppliers. Other leading global industrial and technology leaders, like Apple, have come to rely on cutting-edge components supplied by Japanese partners to power their products.

Even so, the first breakthrough that most foreigners need to make in dealing effectively with the Japanese is to get beyond the communications barriers and their formal manners—their

Tokyo Metropolitan Building in Tokyo. The building houses the headquarters of the Tokyo Metropolitan Government, which governs twenty-three wards and municipalities.

visible kata. Their etiquette is seductively attractive to many Westerners, often impressing them to the point that they become entranced and lose some of their critical faculties, especially their ability to discern between form and substance.

This alone is enough to account for many of the problems that foreigners have in relationships with Japanese. Americans in particular are often susceptible to being overly influenced by stylized, elegant behavior, no doubt subconsciously relating such "good manners" to refinement and a high level of ethics and morality.

A leveling factor has been the introduction to corporate Japan of the Governance Code and other mechanisms of shareholder capitalism. Companies, particularly the ones actively engaged in overseas business, have realized they need to be a lot more transparent and open if they are to become crucial parts of the global supply chain. And more and more of the smaller companies whose operations and shipments remain limited to the domestic market are keen to break out, establishing solid ties with counterparts in the faster growing markets in Asia and elsewhere.

There is neither equality nor Western-style fairness in Japan's traditional, hierarchical, and exclusive culture. Everyone is inherently unequal by design. The demands of the global supply chain require new, more flexible attitudes.

Yet since many Japanese are not experienced in working with other people on an equal basis, as true partners, most of their joint ventures with foreign companies either fail completely after a few years or become disjointed.

One long-time expatriate businessman in Japan observed, obviously after having had some unhappy experience: "You can work for the Japanese or they can work for you, but you cannot work with them."

These factors generally apply to all relationships with typical Japanese, but there are numerous exceptions on an individual as well as a company basis. Still, warn both Japanese and foreign veterans, the best approach in any proposed relationship is to take nothing for granted, and follow the best advice available.

Sometimes, the most effective strategy when dealing with Japanese who want something from you is to make no effort whatsoever to adapt to the Japanese Way. This tends to throw them off balance, break up their line, and weaken their defenses. This approach is more likely to work when your meetings take place away from their offices—and usually the further you are from their home turf, the better off you are.

Generally the ideal approach in dealing with Japanese is a combination of Japanese etiquette and Western or American techniques. Japanese protocol is fine in helping to set the stage for meetings and negotiations. Exchanging business cards, bowing, making polite talk, and developing personal ties all contribute to harmony and feelings of goodwill, and are, in fact, pleasant experiences.

But nothing beats the rational, fact-based, and fair approach to business, diplomatic, and personal relationships that are the bedrock of the American way, and a principle that the Japanese understand, appreciate, and are gradually absorbing into their own culture.

In the ongoing trend for the East and West to work ever closer together, IT and IT devices are now the chief role players. Being culturally neutral, they are inexorably weaning the Japanese from their kata-bound culture.

Index

Photo Credits

Front cover vichie81/depositphotos.com; **Page 2** © Ladda Tonglo/Shutterstock.com; **Page 12** © Neale Cousland/Shutterstock.com; **Page 18** © Komissar007/Shutterstock.com; **Page 23** © wong yu liang/Shutterstock.com; **Page 27** © Wikimedia Commons; **Page 36** © Shirototoro/Dreamstime.com; **Page 38** © Deenida/Dreamstime.com; **Page 46** © Aleksey Baskakov/Dreamstime.com; **Page 50** © Alfonso de Tomas/Shutterstock.com; **Page 53** © zummolo/Shutterstock.com; **Page 54** © J. Henning Buchholz/Shutterstock.com; **Page 58** © Wikimedia Commons; **Page 61** © posztos/Shutterstock.com; **Page 63** © Aduldej/Shutterstock.com; **Page 66** © maroke/Shutterstock.com; **Page 71** © jesadaphorn/Shutterstock.com; **Page 78** © Woravut30/Shutterstock.com; **Page 83** © Ravil Sayfullin/Shutterstock.com; **Page 85** © Tuzemka/Shutterstock.com; **Page 90** © Shaiith/Shutterstock.com; **Page 99** © Kanisorn Pringthongfoo/Shutterstock.com; **Page 101** © onemu/Shutterstock.com; **Page 103** © Alan C. Heison/Shutterstock.com; **Page 105** © marekuliasz/Shutterstock.com; **Page 107** © DK samco/Shutterstock.com; **Page 114** © imtmphoto/Shutterstock.com; **Page 131 top** © Payless Images/Shutterstock.com; **Page 131 bottom** © beeboys/Shutterstock.com; **Page 133** © siro46/Shutterstock.com; **Page 162** © KPG_Payless/Shutterstock.com; **Page 202** © Aleksandar Todorovic/Shutterstock.com; **Page 204** © Stefano Guidi/Shutterstock.com; **Page 210** © superjoseph/Shutterstock.com; **Page 213** © Ugis Riba/Shutterstock.com; **Page 219** © Tooykrub/Shutterstock.com